THE · BEST · OF
Store · Designs 3

THE · BEST · OF
Store·Designs 3

From the National Retail Merchants Association and the Institute for Store Planners' Store Interior Design Competition

PBC INTERNATIONAL, INC. • New York

Distributor to the book trade in the United States:

Rizzoli International Publications, Inc.
597 Fifth Avenue
New York, NY 10017

Distributor to the art trade in the United States:

Letraset USA
40 Eisenhower Drive
Paramus, NJ 07653

Distributor in Canada:

Letraset Canada Limited
555 Alden Road
Markham, Ontario L3R 3L5, Canada

Distributed throughout the rest of the world by:

Hearst Books International
105 Madison Avenue
New York, NY 10016

ISSN 0894-6132

ISBN 0-86636-051-4

Color separation, printing, and binding
by Toppan Printing Co. (H.K.) Ltd., Hong Kong

Typesetting by Vera-Reyes, Inc.

Printed in Hong Kong
10 9 8 7 6 5 3 2 1

Publisher	**Herb Taylor**
Project Director	**Cora Sibal Taylor**
Executive Editor	**Virginia Christensen**
Editor	**Wanda P. Jankowski**
Art Director	**Richard Liu**
Production Manager	**Kevin Clark**

CONTENTS

FOREWORD

We are pleased to announce the publication of **THE BEST OF STORE DESIGNS 3.**

The stores presented in this book have several characteristics in common. Each embodies and exhibits the development of a unique character or image for the store, a thoughtful attention to detail, the careful blending of choice materials to achieve the desired effects, and space and merchandise display planning in which the comfort and needs of the customer are highest priorities.

It was the superb coordination of these characteristics by talented and creative designers and design firms that moved the panel of judges to honor the 24 entries included here with awards.

We hope you will enjoy THE BEST OF STORE DESIGNS 3. It is a valuable reference tool and source for design ideas and visual concepts.

INTRODUCTION

The favorable response to THE BEST OF STORE DESIGNS 2 from retail store planners, designers, design firms and schools has encouraged us to make available once again a collection of the ISP/NRMA Store Interior Design Competition winners.

THE BEST OF STORE DESIGNS 3 presents an interesting variety of creative and superior quality designs, ranging from large department stores designed by in-house and outside consultants, to small specialty shops, where every inch of the limited space is used to its maximum merchandising potential. Hard and soft goods stores are included, as well as supermarkets, convenience shops and mass merchandising stores.

We wish to thank Steve Duffy, I.S.P., Chairman of the ISP/NRMA Store Interior Design Competition, for his dedication and hard work, without which this year's program would not have been such a

Bronson of Bronson/Hutensky Developers; Thomas Natalini, corporate merchandising director of Allied Stores Corp.; Gary Jacquemin, A.I.A, vice president of Esser & Jacquemin, Inc., vice president of the Jaeger Division of Hickey Freeman and president of Flink/Wright Design Services; and Harold Leeds, retired chairperson of the graduate department of interior design at Pratt Institute.

A great deal of both general and detailed information is presented in this book. The publication of this book, however, does not constitute an expressed or implied endorsement by the National Retail Merchants Association (NRMA) or by the Institute of Store Planners (ISP) of any particular product, service or firm.

CHAPTER 1

POLO/Ralph Lauren

Store of the Year

New York, New York

Though there are approximately 75 POLO/Ralph Lauren stores around the world, the shop housed in the Rhinelander Mansion at the corner of Madison Avenue and 72nd Street is the only freestanding POLO shop in Manhattan. Ralph Lauren wanted to create a shop on Madison Avenue in a townhouse that would bring back the feeling of Old-World living and shopping. This atmosphere is intended to complement his extensive line of apparel, which blends classical themes with more modern viewpoints.

Gertrude Rhinelander Waldo had the Renaissance revival townhouse built around the turn of the century. The $500,000 cost included a marble staircase, a ballroom and a bowling alley in the basement. Mrs. Waldo decided not to live in the house after it had been completed, and since she could not find a tenant, it remained vacant for the first 30 years of its existence. In more recent years, the first floor had been rented to shopowners.

Over the years, the mansion had deteriorated significantly. After walking through it, before restoration work began, Naomi Leff, the designer of the POLO/Ralph Lauren shop, noted, "Only one ceiling was in good shape. The rest of the building would have to be recreated from a splinter of mahogany paneling here, a scrap of carved plaster there."

The scope of and attention to detail involved in the restoration was enormous. For example, Naomi Leff designed over 90 different crown moldings. Each molding knife was then ground separately. Eighty-two thousand feet of Honduras mahogany was imported to be fashioned into paneling and woodwork that would grace the interior. The same lighting that was to be used in the store was installed in the woodfinisher's shop, so that all the craftsmen could match their work.

In striving to recreate the environment of a great country house, polished floors, fish trophies, Persian rugs, model boats, old photographs and fresh flowers are scattered throughout the townhouse to promote a home-like feeling. The shop employs a staff of 190, uses a sophisticated security system and cost over $14 million.

Naomi Leff has designed numerous POLO/Ralph Lauren stores. One of the most recent, in addition to the Madison Avenue townhouse shop, is the POLO/Ralph Lauren store on Place Madelaine in Paris, France.

The outstanding craftsmanship and design of the restoration, the attention to detail, the creation of an image reflecting perfectly the quality and style of the merchandise, the blending of unified themes with variety among the store's departments, and the thoughtful consideration of customer comfort has garnered the POLO/Ralph Lauren shop the Grand Prize, Store of the Year Award in the ISP/NRMA Store Interior Design Competition.

POLO/Ralph Lauren New York, New York

FIRST AWARD, Soft Goods Specialty Store, New or Renovated & Grand Prize

Designer: **Naomi Leff and Associates**
New York, New York

Preservation and Restoration of a Landmark

It was the intent of POLO/Ralph Lauren to create a retail environment which reflected the elegant lifestyle of the merchandise. POLO/Ralph Lauren is located in the Rhinelander Mansion, a National Registry building, built in 1889 on Madison Avenue. The adaptation of this building for a retail environment required a tremendous commitment to preserve the remaining outstanding interior ornamental details and to reconstruct the exterior of the building.

The base building, which had been blighted over the years, had to be extensively renovated. Life-safety and building code requirements had to be satisfied. The building systems and means of egress had to be integrated. So as not to disturb the existing ornamental plaster ceilings, the floors above were removed and the lighting and sprinklers were dropped in. Existing wood ceilings, where possible, were removed, restored and reinstalled. Layers of gypsum board were applied to existing wood joists to provide the required fire rating, and sprinklers were placed between the joists.

Because of the potentially high wattage per square foot required for retail use, a low-voltage lighting system was used wherever possible. Since the elaborate plaster ceilings were built against the building floor structure, the ductwork for the HVAC system could not be installed above those ceilings. Consequently, two machine rooms have been installed—one in the lower level and one in the roof hip—to eliminate as much vertical penetration as possible. An intricate and creative design was developed to run the ductwork behind the crowns of the fixture work.

Significant restoration of the existing architectural ornamentation has been done, including the casting and reconstruction of plaster details. Where mahogany wood paneling existed, it has been stripped of layers of paint and restained. Hand-carved ornamental and decorative features have been matched to the few existing architectural clues. Partitions have been designed to reestablish the scale and geometry of the ravaged interior. The planning issues have been used to recreate a residential scale to the space.

Elegance Combined with Accessibility

The store is planned, organized and designed to appeal to the customer and to enhance ease and accessibility of shopping. The first two floors are dedicated to the Men's Collection, with the addition of gift items. Using wood mahogany paneling, the Men's Collection reflects an English haberdashery. A hand-carved balustrade on the monumental paneled stair leading to the Second Floor is a major focal point.

The third floor is devoted to Women's Ready-to-Wear and Accessories. The lighter ambience contrasts with that of the lower levels. Separate areas are devoted to distinctive groups of merchandise, i.e., Collection, Roughwear, Activewear, Shoes.

The fourth floor contains Home Furnishings. The space is anchored by several lifestyle rooms which are designed seasonally as the New Home Furnishings Collections are introduced.

To date, sales have surpassed anticipated projections.

Project: POLO/Ralph Lauren
Location: New York, New York
Client: Ralph Lauren/POLO
Design Firm: Naomi Leff and Associates New York, New York

INTERIOR DESIGN TEAM:

Design Team: Stephen Lomicka, Meg Macleod, Jonathan Halper, Molly Reid, Mary Foley, Beulah Schmitz, Francis Shiu, Joel Harper, Carolina Ieney, Vinod Dadarkar, Wilson Chung
President/Chairman and Project Manager: Naomi Leff
Contractors: E.W. Howell Co. (general), Adler & Nielson Co., Inc. (structural steel), Amberg & Hinzman (cabinetry), Dover Elevator Co. (elevators), A.D. Winston Corp. (HVAC), Colonial Art Decorators, Inc. (painting)

Suppliers: Morell-Brown Plastering Corp. (lath & plaster), The Modern Bronze Foundry (French sandcasting of balusters), Sullivan-Questal (wood carver), Pietra Dura, Inc. (stone sculptor), Norbert Belfer Lighting Mfg. Co. (custom lighting), Gundolt Carpet Workroom (carpet installation), Noris Metal (metal work), Howard Kaplan (bathroom hardware), Cornell Creations (brass work), Sara Balbach (signage)
Photographer: David Phelps

A significant amount of casting and reconstruction of plaster details has been done. Hand-carved features have been matched to existing architectural details.

Men's and Women's Collections and Home Furnishings are displayed throughout four levels of the mansion.

Special services offered to the shop's customers include custom tailoring, monogramming, and coffee or lunch. Dressing rooms are as well-appointed and as comfortable as the sales areas.

The atmosphere of the Men's Collection is that of an English haberdashery. The superior quality of the materials and furnishings—fine wood flooring, paneling and cabinetry, Oriental carpeting, ornate chandeliers—reflects that of the merchandise.

The residential room-like arrangements displaying the home furnishings collection are created through a studied mixture of props and antiques. Props used are not for sale, but many of the antiques and personal accessories scattered throughout the rooms are.

On the fourth floor, the home furnishings collection is arranged as a series of cozy and highly-accessorized vignettes.

The shop creates more than the atmosphere of a great country house. It is a fantasy developed through the skillful blending of the talents of many artists and craftsmen, including sculptors, stone and plaster carvers, brass sandcasters, and woodcarvers. Shown here is the Women's Roughwear area on the third floor.

RUSSIAN AMUSEMENT
CORSICAN
SARGENT
VIRGINIA
The Golden Age

Many of the display cases are antiques which have been restored, refinished, and refitted with hardware.

Some partitions had to be designed to recreate the residential scale of the spaces. Low voltage lighting is used wherever possible.

The paintings, plush seating and fireplace intentionally make the shop seem more like a gracious, stately home. The lifestyle that the products suggest is expressed in the surroundings in which they are displayed.

CHAPTER 2

New Full-Line Department Stores

Efficiency of design and balance among selling, merchandising, and servicing areas are particularly important in full line department stores because of the necessity of dividing the store into departments. Traffic plans should maximize the customer's exposure to all merchandise whether the store is single level or multi-level.

Single level department stores generally require fewer salespeople due to the ability to intersell among departments. The one level store usually has better customer flow distribution, a more flexible floor plan, and more useable space.

The multi-level store also has its advantages. Since the customer's walking time is reduced, overall shopping time is reduced as well. Similar merchandise types can be placed in close proximity to encourage mutual sales.

All department stores, whether they are single or multi-level, must integrate in style and quality with other stores in the chain, while adapting to the particular needs of the climate, and surrounding environment.

The challenge for the design team for Macy's Galleria, Dallas, was to maintain a continuity in merchandise planning and layerage with other established Macy's stores, while instilling a new, fresh look, through combinations of materials and colors that would appeal to the sophisticated Dallas shopper.

The design solution favors a traditional motif, using exotic wood veneers, chandeliers, marble, etched glass, and warm vibrant colors that reflect the climate. This is in contrast to the prototypical Macy's blending of chrome and glass.

Departments flow freely from one to another, distinguished through colors, materials, and uplit ceiling valances.

Parisian's location in the Riverchase Galleria, the Southeast's largest enclosed shopping center, maintains the store's high standing as the South's preeminent retailer. The flagship store is designed around a central core called Parisian Plaza which unites the two-level interior space from within. Architectural elements depicted in the large and colorful "Parisian Point of View" mural are repeated in the actual architectural details of the store's interior.

Smooth circulation is encouraged by the short aisle segments which eliminate uninteresting views of long aisles. The high quality of the merchandise and service is reflected in the fine materials chosen to adorn the store—natural fibers, mahogany, oak, suedes, leathers, and marbles.

Rich's flagship store, also located in the Riverchase Galleria, has been designed to be consistent with the atmosphere and layout of the mall. The interior design theme recalls a classic Southern formality.

The exterior of the main entrance is reminiscent of an antebellum portico, with its lavish cast stone columns. The focal point of the interior is a three-storey escalator well, bounded by large round columns of American sycamore and capped by a domed skylight. Round shapes in subtle rose and cream colors are used throughout the store, and accented by cream marfil, floriant rose, and verde marbles.

Macy's, Dallas Galleria

Dallas, Texas

Parisian

Hoover, Alabama

Rich's Riverchase

Hoover, Alabama

Macy's Galleria Dallas, Texas

FIRST AWARD, New Full Line Department Store

Designer: WalkerGroup/CNI
New York, New York

Upgrading the Image

Objectives for the design of the 256,000-square-foot R.H. Macy store, located in the prestigious Galleria Mall of Dallas, included:

- Upgrading the established Macy's design approach to the discerning Dallas market's level of sophistication
- Adapting Macy's merchandising style to the architectural geometry of the existing mall site
- Establishing continuity with previous Macy's stores in merchandise planning, floor layerage, and major design elements, while departing from those stores in the ensemble of lighting, colors, materials and overall plan.

The designers collaborated with Macy's Store Design, Store Planning and Construction Departments.

The prototypical Macy's chrome and glass design theme is transposed into a more traditional motif of exotic wood veneers, chandeliers, marble, etched glass and a palette of warm, vibrant colors which reflect the climate. A barrel-vaulted skylight made of glass etched with coffer designs crowns the escalator atrium and allows natural light to penetrate into all three selling floors.

The T-shaped main aisles on each of the three floors are easily accessible through three mall entrances, three parking garage entrances and one street door. This adaptive plan combines the linear quality of earlier Macy's plans with the broadside mall-entrance of the Dallas site.

Colors and Materials Establish Department Boundaries

Departments flow freely from one to another. Boundaries are established exclusively through distinctions in colors and materials and in the formal qualities of the sculptured, uplighted ceiling valance. The adjacency between departments, or "layerage," is reminiscent of previous Macy's stores.

On the main floor, curvilinear architecture, including fluted 10-foot columns, is enhanced by accents of polished Swiss pearwood, polished steel, brushed bronze and marble floors.

On the second floor, softly rounded ceiling coves stretch majestically over the Clubhouse, which is located in the main rotunda. A distinctive gallery of designer boutiques is gracefully sheathed in glass throughout the floor.

The third level, the "home fashions" floor, offers a magnificent view of the barrel-vaulted skylight. On this floor, the world-famous "Cellar" is found with its splendid cluster of shops set in a marble-floored mini-mall that features etched glass "store fronts" and is illuminated by Giradelli-style lights.

The heightened appeal to the upscale customer is achieved through the successful coordination of many well-planned elements: the pastel color spectrum, the sumptuous materials and fixtures, the matching of floor with ceiling treatments, and the consideration given to the Galleria site. The R.H. Macy store embodies not only a new image for the renowned company, but reflects an advancement in the state of the art of retail design.

Project:	Macy's Galleria, Dallas
Location:	Dallas, Texas
Client:	R.H. Macy Corporation
Design Firm:	WalkerGroup/CNI New York, New York

INTERIOR DESIGN TEAM:

Planner:	Gale Barter
Designer:	Tom Tarnowski
Decorator:	Kathryn Murray
Project Manager:	Errol Minto
Partner in Charge:	Lawrence J. Israel, F.I.S.P.
President/Chairman:	Kenneth H. Walker, I.S.P.
Consultant:	John Siacca (lighting)
Contractors:	Modern Woodcraft, Versi Craft Corp., Crafted Cabinets, Inc. (perimeters); HBSA Industries, Inc. (showcases)

Suppliers: S. Harris & Co., High Design Group, Innovations, Kranet Fabrics, Laue Wallcoverings, Maharani Fabrics, Markis/Rolon Assoc., William F. Marshall, Patterson Fabrics, Payne Fabrics, Westgate, Willowtex (wallcoverings); Formica, Laminart Inc., Nevamar, Wilsonart (laminates); Robert Allen Fabrics, Ametex, Brunschwig & Fils, Cohama Specifier, Bill Corry, Wolf Gordon, S. Harris & Co., Kravet, Lackawanna Leather, Jack Lennor Larsen, Laue Wallcoverings, Patterson Piazza, Scalamandre, F. Schumacher, Unika Vaev, Waverley Fabrics (fabrics); Clodan Carpet, Couristan, Durkan, S. Harris & Co., Nevamar, Innovations, Weave-Tuft (floor coverings); Banks Stone (stone); Country Floors, Dal Tile, Design Technics, Elon Tile, Innovative Tile (ceramic tile); Indy Lighting, Lightron of Cornwall (lighting); Marvin Walker Assoc. (glass); Gold Leaf & Metallic Powders, Robert Kreuman & Assoc., Laue Wallcoverings (metal)

Photographer: Richard Payne: Houston, Texas

Each of the floors contains a T-shaped main aisle. The store is easily accessible from three mall entrances, three parking garage entrances and one street door.

POLO
POLO

Darker background colors are used in the Men's clothing areas. The consistent design themes used throughout the store occur here: glass enriched displays, wood trims and coffered ceilings. Track-lighted displays are simple to allow attention to be focused on the merchandise.

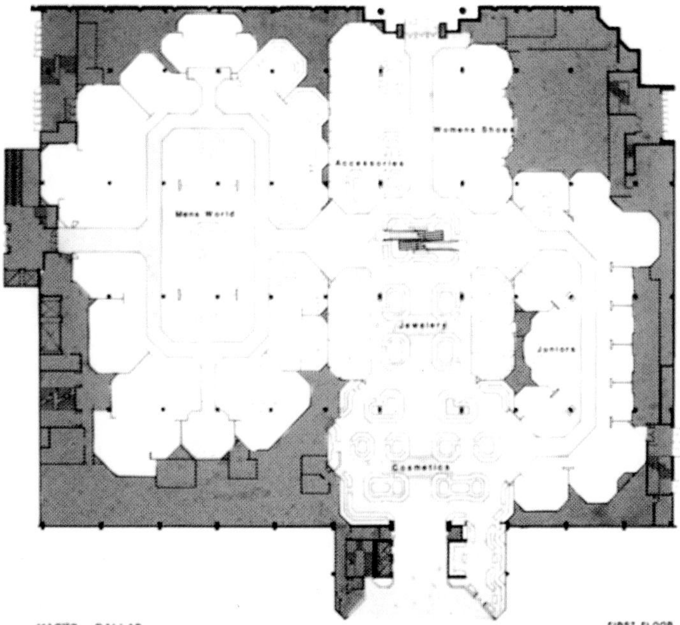

MACYS DALLAS FIRST FLOOR

YSL
OPIUM

The palette of warm, vibrant colors reflects the climate. The stepped ceiling mimics the angular display-case wall configurations.

Stepped ceilings add interest to the jewelry department. Wood and marble create a traditional motif, in contrast to the more modern, prototypical Macy's chrome and glass design theme.

swatch

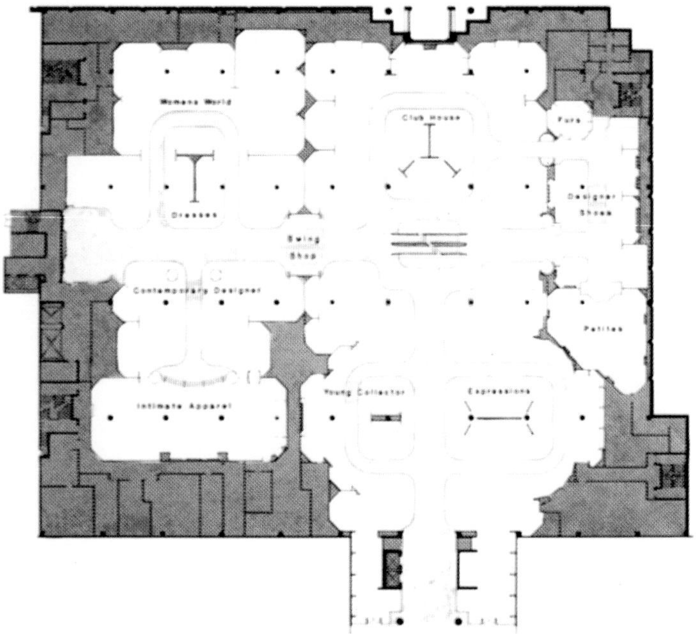

Softly rounded ceiling coves stretch over the Clubhouse in the second floor's main rotunda. The distinctive designer boutiques scattered throughout the floor are sheathed in glass.

LITTLE SHOPS

The rounded shapes and lines of display settings and columns are echoed in the curved ceiling formations. Departments flow freely from one to another, and are established exclusively through variations in colors, materials and in the sculptured quality of the uplighted ceiling valances.

Track lights are used to focus on and to add punch to displays. Glass panels serve a dual purpose: they set off and partially enclose displays and clearly bear the names of departments or designers in each area.

Parisian

Hoover, Alabama

HONORABLE MENTION, New Full Line Department Store

Designer: Schafer Associates
Oak Brook, Illinois

Parisian Point of View

The Riverside Galleria, located just outside Birmingham, is the Southeast's largest enclosed shopping center. This location was chosen for Parisian's flagship store to maintain the store's standing as the South's preeminent retailer. Parisian reflects the character of the community—a city of contrasts, a blend of the old and the new—by incorporating a regional expression in the interior architecture. Since Birmingham is the retailer's home base, it was important to express clearly and strongly the "Parisian Point of View."

The building is designed around a dramatic center core, "Parisian Plaza," which is a meeting place and a stage for special events. Parisian Plaza unites the two-level interior space from within and becomes the dominant entrance to the mall. An integral part of the Plaza is a mural entitled "Parisian Point of View," which works with the structural elements within the space.

Short Aisle Segments Aid Traffic Flow

The interior is designed to promote easy traffic flow throughout the entire store and to expose the customer to all departments. Aisles are shaped and faceted in short segments to encourage smooth circulation and to provide the opportunity for more merchandise to be viewed along the aisle. This system eliminates views of long runs of uninteresting aisles.

Rich materials such as natural fibers, mahogany and oak woods, suedes, leathers and marbles are used to reflect the high quality of merchandise and service for which Parisian is known. Details are well thought out, from floor to ceiling; there is a cohesiveness of design and materials. Throughout the store, patterns highlight special departments: marble flooring graces the Parisian Room, vinyl flooring insets resembling a hopscotch game contrast with white ceramic tile in "Parisian Kids," and a subtle ceramic tile floor pattern in the center core is repeated on the mall entrance walls.

Project:	Parisian
Location:	Hoover, Alabama
Client:	Parisian, Inc.
Design Firm:	Schafer Associates Oak Brook, Illinois

INTERIOR DESIGN TEAM:

Planner:	Bob Schafer
Designer:	Charles Sparks
Decorator:	Michelle Barnard
Job Captain:	George Zachotina
Project Manager:	John Salemi
Partner in Charge:	Bob Schafer
President/Chairman:	Bob Schafer
Consultants:	David L. Peacher, A.I.A. (architect), Bob Carlson, Lithonia Lighting (lighting)
Contractors:	Brasfield & Gorrie (general), Raines Bros., Inc. (perimeter), American Woodcraft (miscellaneous loose fixtures), Greenwood Fixture & Display (showcase), Fixplay Display (glass cube units), Chandelite, Inc. (casework)
Photographer:	Jim Norris

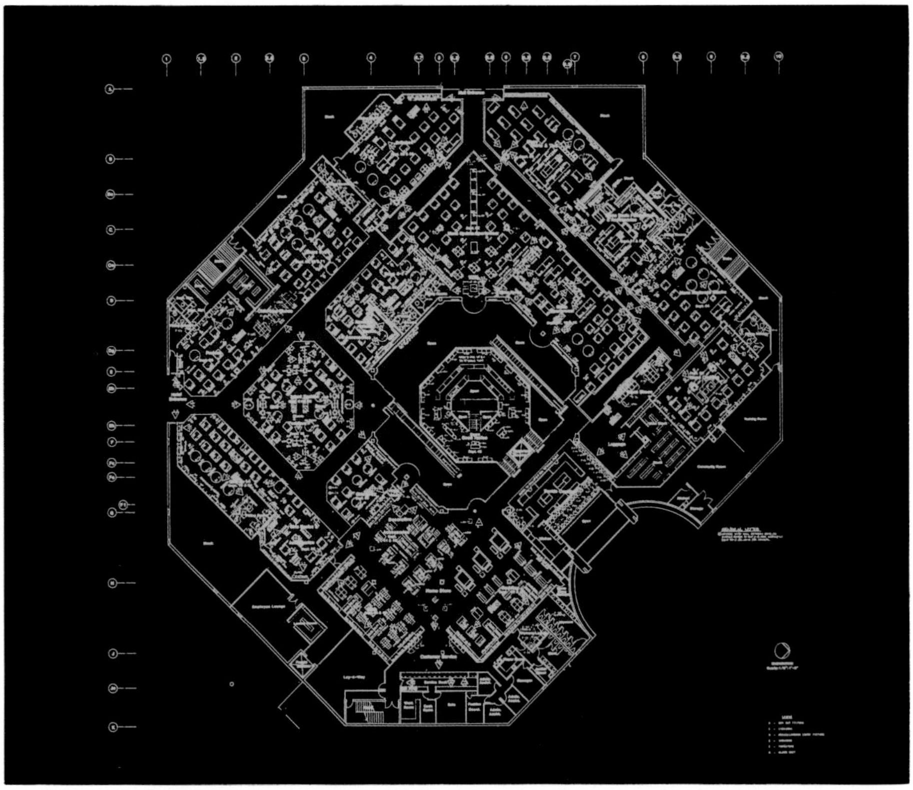

Aisle segments are kept short to eliminate views of long, uninteresting aisles. The two-level store is entered from Parisian Plaza. Escalator and stairwell are readily visible at the entrance for shoppers' convenience.

Simple, yet effective design details—vinyl insets contrasted with white ceramic tile, and suspended pastel-colored clouds—create a lively, atmosphere in the Parisian Kids department.

An attention-getting display is positioned in the aisle. The checkered flooring, high-tech catwalk holding casually-posed mannequins and streamlined lighting fixtures suspended from slim black rods create a modern look in the young women's sportswear area.

ESPRIT
ESPRIT

The short aisle segments allow the customer to see a wide range of merchandise. The multi-leveled displays create interest as the shopper's eyes are drawn from the lowest level upward.

A delicate, romantic display highlights "The Finer Things" lingerie section. The merchandise is clearly visible from and directed toward the main aisle. Columns and archways reflect the feeling of traditional Southern elegance.

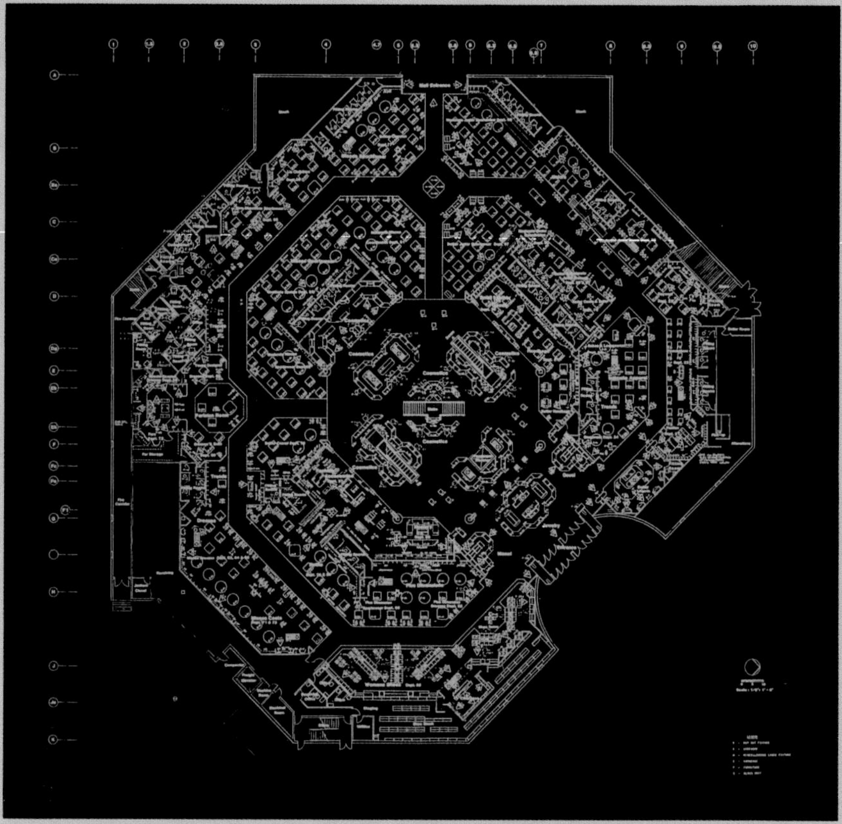

The interior architecture has a regional flavor. The gracefully curved balconies and archways depicted in the colorful mural are echoed in actual architectural details throughout the store.

The uplighted ceiling and light-colored flooring contrast with the darker shades of the merchandise and background colors in the Men's Clothing department.

Rich's Riverchase Hoover, Alabama

HONORABLE MENTION, New Full Line Department Store

Designer: Hambrecht Terrell International
New York, New York

Anchor Store Integrated into Galleria

Rich's new flagship store is located in the Riverchase Galleria, outside Birmingham, Alabama. The location itself influenced the store's overall image. As one of two major anchor stores in the most important shopping mall to open in Alabama in many years, the exterior architecture and interior design had to be consistent with the rest of the mall.

The mall is constructed on the century-old architectural concept of the galleria, which mingles commerce with living and working environments. It is a glass-enclosed, 1,300-foot city park which strives to recreate "Main Street." No ordinary department store would fit within such a context.

Classic Southern Formality

The design theme projected for the store recalls classic Southern formality. On the exterior, this is carried out through the use of lavish cast stone columns and an entrance reminiscent of an antebellum portico. Lighting also reinforces this formality. Two shafts of light frame the store's entrance; in the evening, the windows are illuminated to beckon the customer inside.

The store's interior reflects the use of formal architectural elements. A dramatic three-storey escalator well is contained by large round columns of American sycamore, supporting a domed skylight above. Strong and structural in design, it dominates the shopper's eye and provides a central focal point for each of the three floors.

The strength of the interior architecture is softened by rounded shapes in subtle colorations of roses and creams, accentuated by crema marfil, floriant rose and verde marbles. Additional architectural elements of American sycamore add to the warmth of the environment.

In the spirit of a stately home, there is no glaring signage on the front of the store. A subtle sign is positioned on the building's side. Trees have been planted throughout the parking area to create a pleasant plaza effect.

Project:	Rich's Riverchase
Location:	Riverchase Mall Hoover, Alabama
Client:	Rich's, Inc. Atlanta, Georgia
Design Firm:	Hambrecht Terrell International New York, New York

INTERIOR DESIGN TEAM:

Planner:	Emil Montero
Designer:	Bryan Gailey
Decorators:	John Hoch, Gregory Tice
Job Captain:	Marian D'Oria
Project Manager:	Emil Montero
Partner in Charge:	Edward C. Hambrecht
President/Chairman:	James E. Terrell, Edward C. Hambrecht
Consultants:	David A. Mintz (lighting); Syska & Hennessey, Reiffman & Blum (mechanical)
Contractor:	Dunn Construction
Suppliers:	Merchandise Equipment Co., Crown Store Equipment, Anton Waldmann Associates, Hughes & Co. (fixtures); Bigelow, Karastan, Amazonian Woods (flooring)
Photographer:	John Wadsworth, Norfolk, Virginia

The curved, overhanging entryway is a harbinger of the classic, formal approach to the design of the store's interior. The main entrance is unencumbered by signage, which is subtly placed at the side of the building.

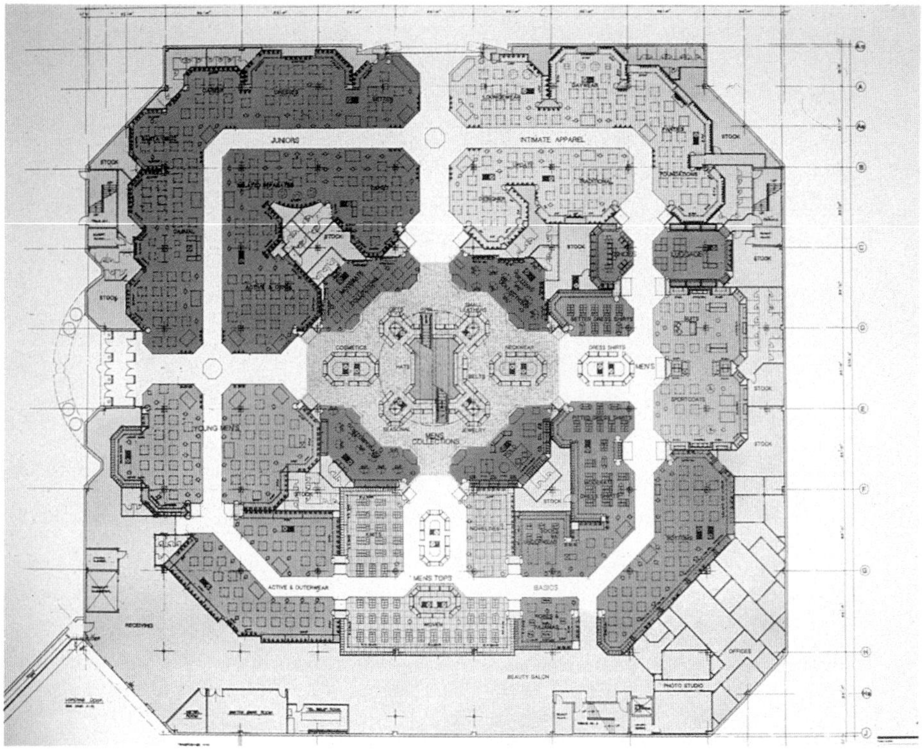

The edges of the Men's Department are defined by a striking yellow strip of marble embedded in the floor and a matching, continuous ceiling-recessed line of light outlining the perimeter of the yellow overhang.

Pink marble and floral displays create a feminine aura in the Fragrance Department on the first floor. The angular pattern of the ceiling is repeated in the shape of the display case below. The lighting is unobtrusive.

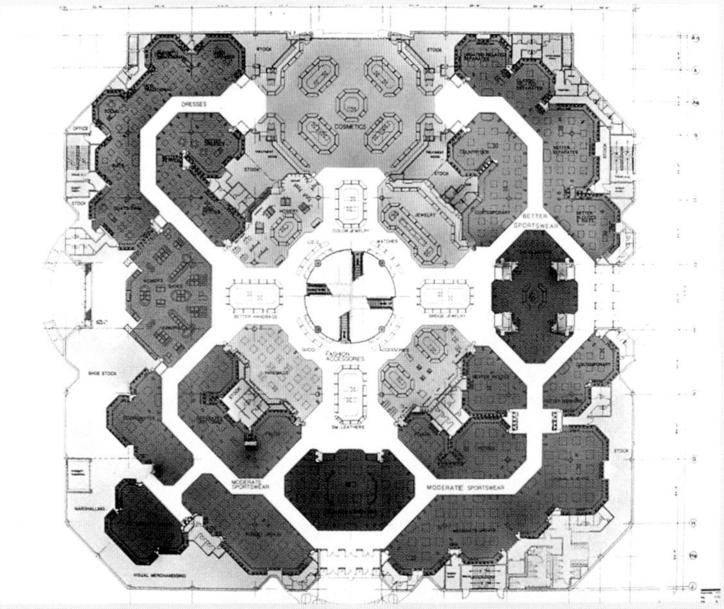

A marble aisle encircles the perimeter of the Ladies' Ready-to-Wear Department. Its shape is echoed in the illuminated cove above. Casually-posed mannequins are an eye-catching focal point placed at the intersection of the aisles.

Fine wood display cases, and brown and golden colored marble floors create an appropriate masculine atmosphere for the Men's Accessories area in the escalator well. The openness of the displays makes the merchandise easily accessible.

HOFFRITZ

The illuminated ceiling cove adds a feeling of spaciousness to the promenade in the Marketplace. Unifying elements used throughout the gallery of mini-shops include the black and white checkerboard pattern featured in the floor tile and in a border above the display windows, and the repetition of round, blue columns.

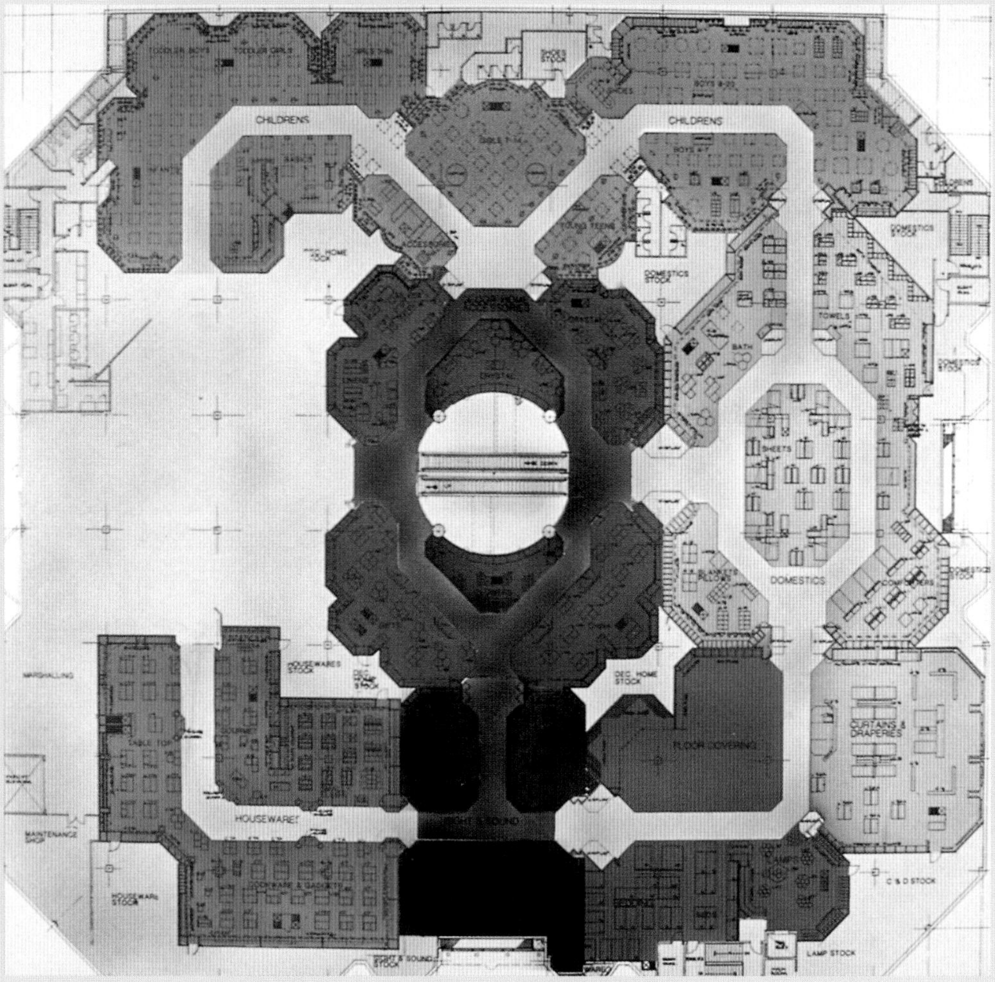

CHAPTER

3

Renovated Full-Line Department Stores

Planning and designing a renovation is different from new store design in several ways. Generally, renovation is undertaken to solve existing problems, and greater budgetary restrictions may apply. Physical limitation are increased; designers must deal with existing, permanent aspects of the structure.

The reasons for embarking on a renovation are also varied. The look and layout of a store may need updating to complement changes in merchandise, or type or quantity of customers. Flaws in the efficiency of the store's original plan may require correcting. Increased local competition may prompt a desire for change. All three stores in this chapter have undergone major revamping.

Belk's Southpark flagship store had to establish a new upscale corporate image. Major architectural changes have been made, including the conversion of a previously unused storage floor to selling space, and the installation of a new escalator well capped by a double-vaulted skylight.

The entire store has been reorganized to promote smooth circulation and sensible department adjacencies. Each floor is identified by its own strong design themes, which rely heavily on rich colors and materials. An increase in merchandise visibility has been accomplished by pushing department widths to the maximum along the aisles, and maintaining minimum department depth.

The interior of Carson Pirie Scott & Co. has also been replanned. Merchandise classification productivity was reevaluated and led to the expansion, intensifying and updating of the core businesses on the two levels of the store. Sameness has been minimized mainly through the creation of varied environments in each department. Good aisle exposure for merchandise, and simple interior architecture reinforce the intention that the merchandise, rather than the decor or the architecture, be the message.

The single level Hess's store had become dated and outmoded, and so a plan has been devised which pulls together all the disparate elements that had interfered with the presentation of a unified image. A formal aisle system unites the departments, which are organized into distinct "worlds" and are arranged in a logical order. Each world has its own particular character. For example, highly lacquered black columns line aisles and support the grid-like overhangs which dominate the center of the floor in the Men's section. The high-spirited Junior World has a black-painted ceiling ringed by contrasting white neon. Red space frames are also used to house merchandise and for decoration.

Renovation design involves a balancing and blending of a complex variety of factors. Elements of the store's design and structure which remain unchanged must integrate with newly-planned improvements in circulation and traffic flow, visibility and accessibility of merchandise, positioning of displays, and careful placement of department adjacencies, to project a fresh, and unified image.

Belk's Southpark
Charlotte, North Carolina

Carson Pirie Scott & Co.
North Riverside, Illinois

Hess's
Lehigh County, Pennsylvania

Belk's Southpark Charlotte, North Carolina

FIRST AWARD, Renovated Full Line Department Store

Designer: Hambrecht Terrell International
New York, New York

Escalator Well Capped by Double-Vaulted Skylight

As the flagship store for a large regional chain of department stores, Belk's Southpark in Charlotte, North Carolina, defines a new upscale, corporate image. Major architectural changes include an unused storage floor that has been converted for selling and a new escalator well capped by a double-vaulted skylight that ties the four selling floors together.

The entire store has been reorganized for easy circulation and good departmental adjacencies. The lower level and fourth floor contain home merchandise; the main and third floors house fashions.

An axial circulation system is employed to ease shopping. Each floor has a strong, individual design theme. The lower level contains a gallery of shops that flank a marble promenade in a slate and creme diagonal checkerboard pattern. Mahogany paneling leads into dramatic, individualized departments. Rich colors, such as Prussian blue for Tabletop, deep pearl for Sight and Sound and mahogany for Housewares, form an interesting backdrop for merchandise display. All is contrasted with creme for freshness.

Individual Design Themes for Each Floor

On the main floor a strong ceiling fixture lights both up and down to define clearly the departments and the circumferential circulation. The ceiling's dome-like effect is in contrast to a small-scaled step detail which is repeated on the perimeters. The ceiling shapes are echoed in floor borders. In each of the departments, the color proportions of the continuous creme-with-charcoal trim theme are changed. All departments are organized for maximum width at the aisle and for minimum depth, with the walls segmented into numerous shop statements.

As one travels up to the fashion floor, the mirror and brass that trim the escalator well are heightened by custom wall sconces on the monumental piers which visually connect the floors and emphasize vertical movement.

The galleria promenade on the fashion floor leads directly into sportswear, where many shop categories and design expressions flank the double loop aisle system. Black marble floored boutiques anchor the escalator well and house seasonal shops. Intimate apparel and dresses each have a soft, well-lit background that sets off the Regency Room, where haute couture is highlighted. The Regency Room, enhanced with verde marble and bronze, is the focal point of the aisle.

On the fourth floor, a central group of domestics shops encircle the escalator wel The merchandise categories are highlightec in room-size glazed show windows. The children's world is simple and whimsical.

The finished store sets a new tone for Belk's. It brings the large flagship store to the forefront of store design, incorporating state-of-the-art merchandise, techniques an lighting. The use of luxurious materials to frame neutral backdrops for merchandise presentations prepares this store for a new generation of affluent shoppers.

Project:	Belk's Southpark
Location:	Charlotte, North Carolina
Client:	Belk Brothers Company
Design Firm:	Hambrecht Terrell International New York, New York

INTERIOR DESIGN TEAM:

Planner:	Art Kramberg
Designer:	Edward Calabrese
Decorator:	Susan Starnes, Karen Kennedy
Job Captain:	Angelo Dascal
Project Manager:	Bernhart Rumphurst
Partner in Charge:	Harve M. Oeslander
President/Chairman:	James E. Terrell, Edward C. Hambrecht
Consultant:	David A. Mintz (lighting)
Contractors:	Anton Waldmann & Associates, H.B.S.A. Industries (perimeters); Carlson Store Fixtures (loose fixtures)
Suppliers:	HGH Design Group; Norton Blumenthal; Laue Wallcovering
Photographer:	John Wadsworth, Norfolk, Virginia

The escalator well, which winds through four floors, is capped by a double-vault skylight.

FURNITURE
LEVEL 4
LEVEL 4

In the Marketplace, glazed room-size windows, and light-colored wood floor and display racks create a country atmosphere for the sumptuous foods and rich candies available.

The escalator well serves as a streamlined backdrop, and richly colored display stands and carpeting provide a dramatic foil for the delicate merchandise.

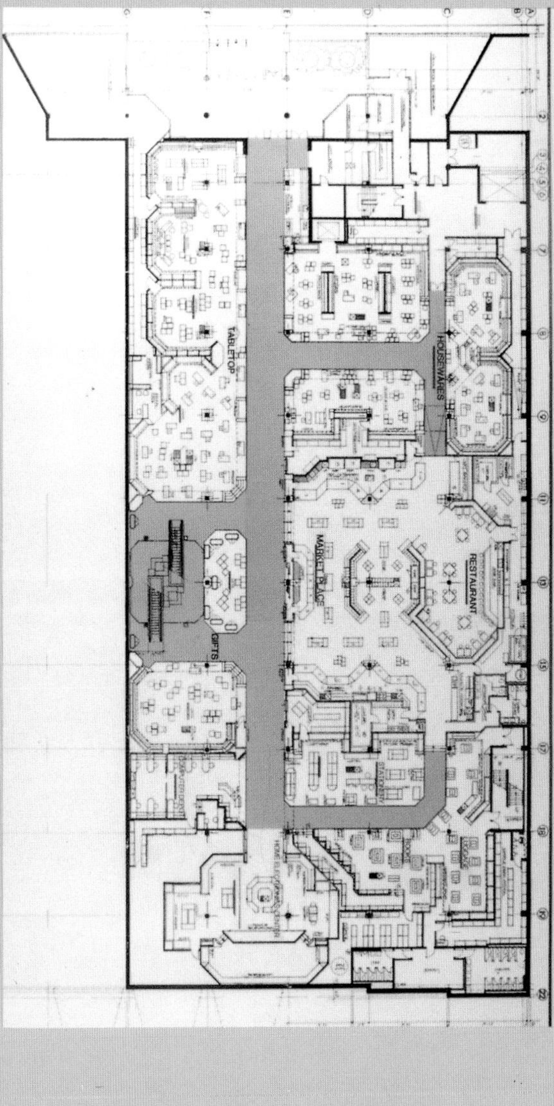

A gallery of housewares shops flanks the aisle, which is patterned with a slate and creme diagonal checkerboard.

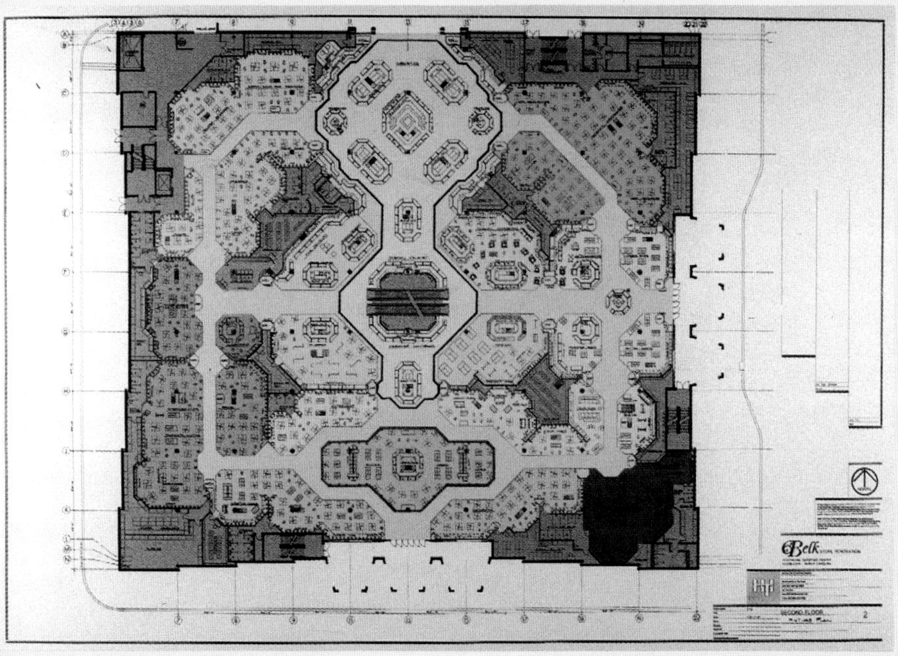

The soft, well-lighted backgrounds of the Intimate Apparel and Women's Dress areas set off the darker drama of the Regency Room behind them. The Regency Room, which features haute couture, is the focal point of the aisle.

The mannequin is playfully positioned in the Women's Shoes section to look into the escalator well. Custom wall sconces are mounted on piers in the well that visually connect the floors and emphasize vertical movement.

ESPRIT
SIGNATURE
GLORIA VANDERBILT

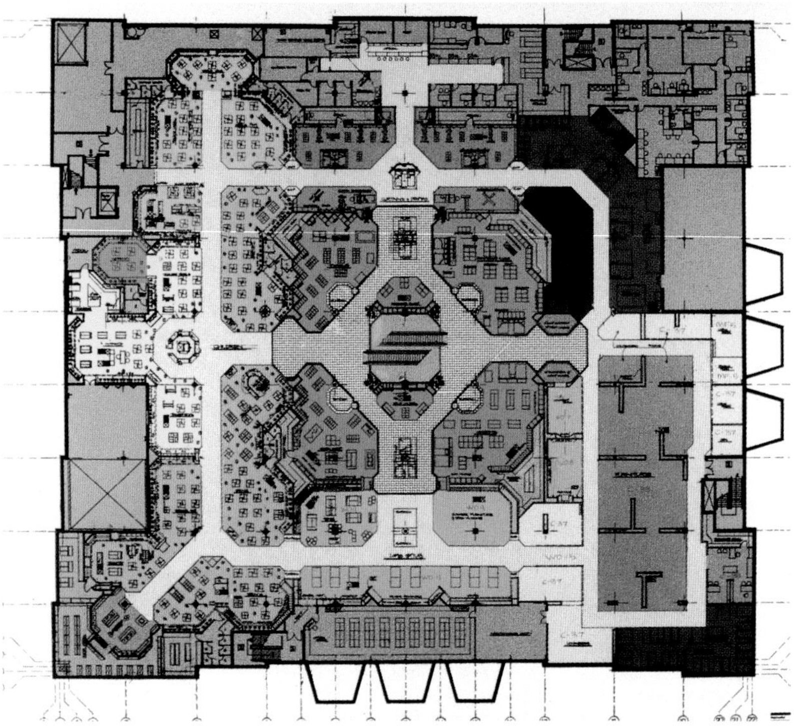

The interesting ceiling shapes in the Young Men's section are echoed in the floor borders below.

The illuminated coved ceiling creates the feeling of greater height. The wood trim adds a masculine touch to the light-colored Men's Sportswear Department.

YOUNG MEN'S

Carson Pirie Scott & Co.

North Riverside, Illinois

HONORABLE MENTION, Renovated Full Line Department Store
Designer: Schafer Associates
Oak Brook, Illinois

Diversity of Merchandise Environments

Carson Pirie Scott & Co. was a store with limited potential for increased market share. No demographic growth was predicted for the area surrounding the store. The challenges for the design firm were to reevaluate classification productivity and to replan and update both levels of the 180,000 square foot unit to expand and intensify the core businesses identified by the client. The objective was to follow a critical path schedule which allowed only six months of phased construction while maintaining sales.

The designers utilize vertical and horizontal space to the maximum. A diversity of merchandise environments has been created in order to strengthen identity among classifications and to minimize sameness. However, the environments demonstrate that the merchandise is the message, not the decor or the architecture.

Simple Interior Architecture

The depth of existing departments has been reduced. The departments are clearly identifiable due to increased aisle exposure. All space within the departments is useable. The interior architecture is simple, emphasizing in-store visual merchandising. A fashion statement is incorporated into both levels.

On a relatively limited budget, all aspects of renovation have been engaged, including a totally new floor plan involving considerable demolition, a new perimeter wall and hardware system, a reworked and updated lighting system, all new floorcoverings and an updated loose floor fixture program. The selling space has been increased through replanning by 11,000 square feet.

Project:	Carson Pirie Scott & Company
Location:	North Riverside, Illinois
Client:	Carson Pirie Scott & Company
Design Firm:	Schafer Associates Oak Brook, Illinois

INTERIOR DESIGN TEAM:

Planners:	Rob Lubben, Bob Schafer
Designers:	Charles Sparks, Stewart Lewis
Decorators:	Leslie Richards, Lynne Gohdes
Project Manager:	Gene Mostowski
Partners in Charge:	Ron Lubben, Charles Sparks
President/Chairman:	Bob Schafer
Contractors:	Pritscher & Erbach (general), Goebel Fixture Co., Bernhard Woodwork (perimeters), Bernhard Woodwork, Torgersen Bros., Inc. (showcases)

Photographer:	Jim Norris
Project:	Hess's
Location:	South Mall Lehigh County, Pennsylvania
Client:	Hess's, A Wholly Owned Subsidiary of Crown American Corporation
Design Firm:	Norwood Oliver Design Associates New York, New York

Glass block columns are the striking centerpieces of the cosmetics showcase islands. The light-colored ceiling, floor and display counters allow the brightly-colored merchandise to attract attention.

Calvin Klein
OBSESSION

ESPRIT

Each department is given maximum aisle exposure and has a shallow depth. The circular column theme used in other departments is continued here, but the atmosphere is more high-tech, reflected in the stark black and white contrasts and TV screens.

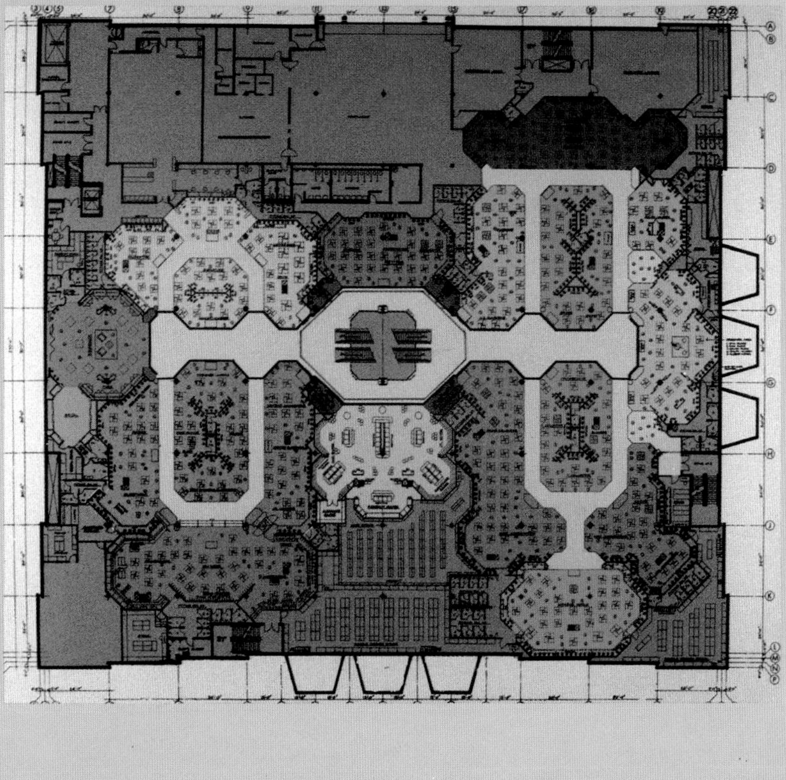

LIZ KIDS
KIDS

Display racks are placed at the aisle's edge for easy viewing. Displays are simple to allow the emphasis to be kept on the merchandise.

The lighting system uses both permanently installed fixtures and adjustable track and downlight units. The monochromatic background makes the boldly colored accenting particularly effective. The display units on wheels can be repositioned conveniently.

Columns and adjoining glass panels are used as backdrops for displays and serve as dividers from one type of merchandise to another in the lingerie department.

A new perimeter wall system and new lighting systems have been installed. Virtually all merchandise is visible from the aisle.

A diversity of environments is created to minimize uniformity and to increase differentiation among merchandise classifications. The contrast between black and white is used differently here than in the ladies' sportwear area. The sleek black ceiling, gray-accented showcases and dark flooring allow the white ceiling above the counter area to become an eye-catching element.

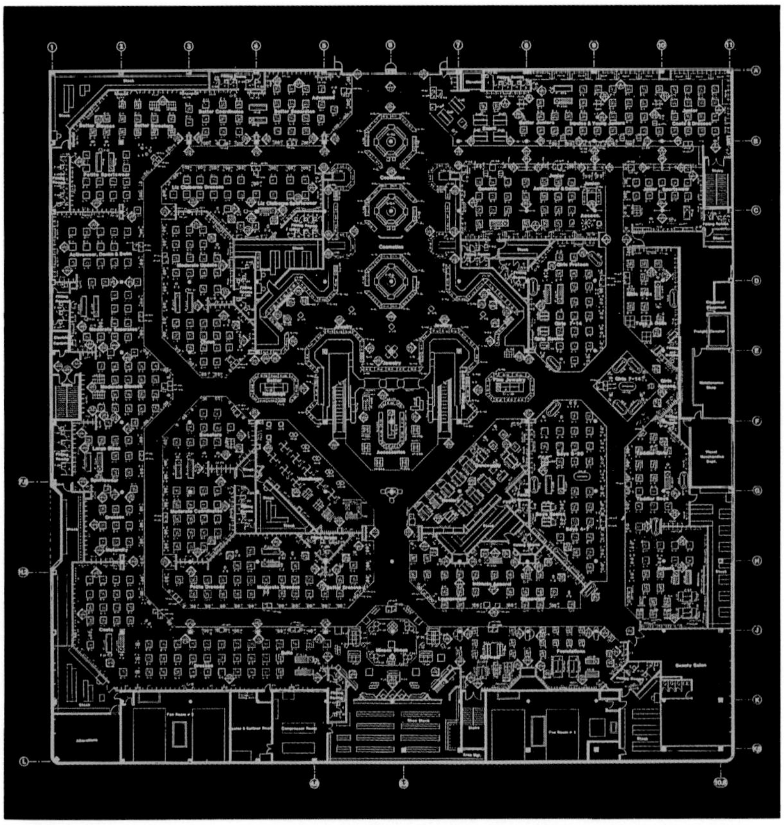

EVATOR

The simplicity of the interior architecture encourages strong in-store visual merchandising emphasis. The masculine tone is created by darker floor coverings, squared columns and grid-like display elements.

Hess's Lehigh County, Pennsylvania

HONORABLE MENTION, Renovated Full Line Department Store

Designer: Norwood Oliver Design Associates
New York, New York

Shopper Transformed into "Worlds" Traveller

The dated and outmoded 100,000-square-foot, one-level Hess store was filled with sprawling, merchandise-packed departments that were due for remodeling. The store has been brought into the 1980's with taste and sophistication by designers who turned to geometry as a tool in pulling together the vast, disparate elements.

A formal aisle system of marble unites the myriad departments which have been organized into tidy, enclosed "Worlds." One World follows another in a natural and logical order. Each World has its own distinctive character and design, while promoting the impression that the entire collection of Worlds is a uniquely balanced whole.

The centerpiece of the Cosmetic and Accessories World is a dazzling, gigantic, Deco-shaped chandelier designed with multiple-stacked beams and made of softly glowing pink rosa mirror that is brilliantly illuminated by hundreds of tiny, twinkling lights. The walls angle back from the ceiling in confection-colored bands with center strips of pink mirror. The result of the masterful orchestration of light, line and form is an environment that is lushly feminine and inviting.

There is an impelling, modern sensibility at work in the Women's World, tempered with a restrained sense of tradition. Neo-classic columned "carousels" punctuate the aisle patterns on either side of the sparkling Contempo department. A sense of refinement results from the blending of these elements with a range of soft brush-stroke colors.

Colors Capture Changing Moods

Entry into the Mens' World and the accompanying change in atmosphere is accomplished in a skillfull, dignified manner. Highly lacquered, gleaming black columns line the aisles and support the grid-like overhang, which dominates the center of the floor. Muted taupes combine with stark white and opaque black to create a striking background for the merchandise.

Designed to be a lavish and exuberant use of space, the high-spirited Junior World has a black-painted ceiling, 13 feet high, ringed and invigorated by contrasting white neon. Red space frames are used as elements of decoration, for local presentation and to house merchandise. These unifying ingredients give the space a vital, soaring quality.

Awash with color and neon, the Childrens' World is a celebration of conviviality and fun. Parents as well as children find patronizing the World a jubilant experience.

In ancillary, but no less important Worlds, it is clear from the attention to details that the designs are well-controlled and unified, while bringing to the shopping environments a sense of exuberance and liveliness.

Vice President in Charge:	Stephen Young, I.S.P.
President/Chairman:	Norwood Oliver, I.S.P.
Contractor:	Wm. Bloom & Sons, Inc.
Photographer:	Norwood Oliver Design in-house personnel

INTERIOR DESIGN TEAM:

Planner:	Ed Allison with Hess's Store Planning Department
Designer:	Stan Kao
Decorator:	Kathy Douglas
Job Captain:	Joe Tormos
Project Manager:	Madan Vazirani, A.I.A., I.S.P.

Red space-frame displays and rings of neon create an atmosphere of exuberance and vitality in the Junior World.

The lighting units that focus intense white light on the display are positioned between the rings of colorful neon.

In the Giftware section, black accents are incorporated into the archways and columns. Ample circulation space is provided for viewing items displayed in the enclosed area beneath the overhang.

The grid-like overhang dominatcs thc aisle. Muted taupes combined with black and white create a striking background.

Highly-lacquered black columns that line the aisles and support the grid-like overhang achieve a masculine flavor appropriate for the Men's World.

The neo-classical style is reflected in the sculptured busts and columns used in the displays that punctuate the aisles in Women's World.

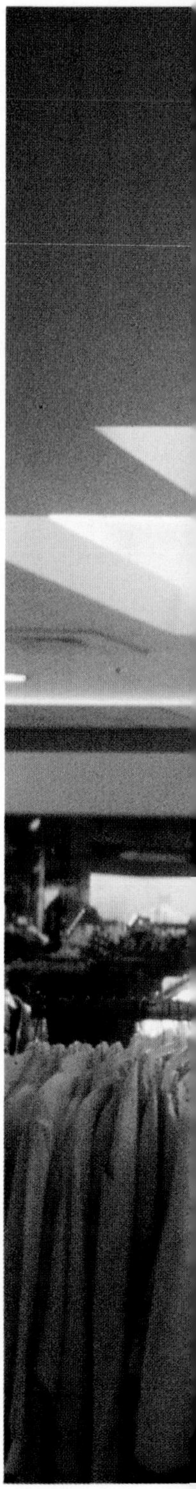

The centerpiece of the Cosmetics and Accessories World is a Deco-style chandelier composed of multiple, stacked beams. The walls angle back from the ceiling highlighted by confection-colored bands with pink-mirror center strips.

A coved ceiling in an eye-catching geometric pattern forms a brightly lit canopy over the women's wear display. Neutral colors provide a soft, nondistracting background for the merchandise.

CHAPTER 4

New Full-Line Department Store Renovations Designed by In-House Staff

Because of their direct and on-going contact with the store, in-house staff involved in a renovation can contribute levels of expertise that an independent consultant cannot. The in-house staff enjoys the advantages of being familiar with the store's structure and limitations, the type of merchandise, the overall direction the store is going in, and the particular needs of the customer in the locale.

The renovated Belk store reflects a mixture of neo-classical and contemporary styling embodied in details such as ceiling drops, custom mouldings, light coves, and architecturally-shaped ceilings. The high-quality materials used add touches of refinement and elegance to the new, updated image of the Belk store. Italian marbles are used in the cosmetics and fashion areas. Soft and natural fabrics are contrasted throughout the store with the high gloss of engraved mirrors, glass walls, and custom stainless steel mouldings.

At Printemps de la Mode, the renovation included the addition of new types of merchandise—women's fashions. The client wanted the design of the Magasin de la Mode to encourage customers to "encounter emotion." Artworks are used to reflect this very special theme, and create a unique visual and shopping experience. Glassed cupolas at crossways, a life-size bust complemented by round-cornered furniture, a floor of Carrara marble, a water-green arch of triumph, and imposing swinging clocks placed at strategic crossways are some of the unusual details.

Whether the renovation involves creating a new image or updating an old one, the in-house staff can use their experiences to advantage by troubleshooting and avoiding problems early on in the planning and design stages.

Belk
Rocky Mount, North Carolina

Printemps de la Mode
Paris, France

Belk Rocky Mount, North Carolina

FIRST AWARD, New Full Line Department Store Designed by In-House Staff

Designer: Belk Stores Services Inc.
Charlotte, North Carolina

Five Retailing Areas on One Level

The 111,785-square-foot, one-level Belk's Store contains the latest retail designs and merchandise presentations tailored to the geographical location. The store is divided into five major retailing sections: Ladies', Accessories, Men's, Children's, and Home Fashions.

On each side of the mall entrance is Ladies' Sportswear and Dresses. The center core features a vaulted ceiling highlighting Ladies' Accessories, Shoes and Cosmetics. The No. 1 exterior entrance introduces Men's Fashions, while the No. 2 exterior entrance leads into Home Furnishings. The No. 3 exterior entrance is near the general office and customer service areas, and adjacent to the children's world.

All the fashion areas are connected by a perimeter aisle that creates good customer flow with easy access to every department. From the perimeter aisle, there are four entryways to the center core, which are easily reached from any area.

The departmental adjacencies and specialized fixtures have been planned to ease the customer in merchandise selection. The walls are flexible and versatile and create visual impact.

A Blend of Neo-Classical and Contemporary

The predominant themes in this store are a blend of neo-classical and contemporary designs unified through the use of ceiling drops, custom mouldings, light coves and architectural shapes. In order to unite the exterior and interior, the black granite used at the entrances is also used on key focal walls in the store. A sénse of drama and elegance is created in the center core by an impressive 120-foot vaulted ceiling with mirrored ends. The vault is lighted by a decorative custom cove and supported by large round columns with capitals. The neo-classical look is continued into the children's area by the use of playful arches, round columns and open trusses in a blend of rich pastels.

A combination of Italian marbles throughout the cosmetic core and fashion areas adds to the richness and elegance of the store. Soft and natural fabrics contrast with the slickness and high gloss of other materials and paints. Colors in the ladies' shop include a range of soft seafoam greens, mauves and peach tones. Frosted-glass accent walls trimmed with copper mouldings continue the blend of neo-classical and contemporary design.

Masculine simplicity is achieved in the men's clothing area by the use of custom mahogany cases and black glass accent walls complemented by the warm gray tones in carpet and paints. Neon, metallic finishes and raised display platforms in juniors' and young men's clothing create a theatrical, dynamic identity. Engraved mirrors, glass walls and custom stainless steel mouldings add an elegant touch. Furnishings and accessories throughout the store have been selected to complete the neo-classical look.

Project: Belk
Location: Rocky Mount, North Carolina
Client: Belk
Design Firm: Belk Stores Services Inc.
Charlotte, North Carolina

INTERIOR DESIGN TEAM:

Planner: Gary L. Mitchell, I.S.P.
Designer: Gail Boggs, A.S.I.D.
Job Captain: James Connell
Department Manager: Robert J. Bramhall, I.S.P.
Chief Architect: Jean G. Surratt, V.P., A.I.A.
Director of Store Planning: Joe H. Robinson, Sr. V.P.

Contractors: Stanly Fixture Company, Inc. (perimeter, loose flooring and showcases); J.C. Moag Corp. (binning and mirrors); Brewer Paint Company (painting)
Photographer: Belk Stores Services, Inc.

Soft, natural fabrics are contrasted with the gloss and slickness of the background paints and materials, such as marble and bronze.

In the Young Men's area, the shape of the raised platform display is repeated in the lowered ceiling. Bold, vertical lettering identifies brand groupings.

The angled glass partitions define edges of the Women's Dress area, while allowing a full view of the merchandise. Frosted glass accent walls are trimmed with copper moulding.

In the Fine Jewelry Department, the neo-classical style is carried through with columns placed on the perimeter of the cove. The 120-foot vaulted ceiling has mirrored ends.

EXIT

The combination of neo-classical and contemporary styles can be seen in the round columns joined by open trusses in the pastel-colored Children's Department.

BOY SCOUTS

A double band of neon runs along the perimeter of the ceiling cove and creates a dynamic, theatrical identity for the Young Men's area.

Black glass accent walls, warm gray tones in carpeting and paints and custom mahogany display cases merge to create an atmosphere of masculine simplicity in the Men's Department.

The stepped ceiling echoes the angular lines of the displays. The rich and vibrant colors of high-quality shoes stand out against a neutral-colored background.

Printemps, Paris, France

HONORABLE MENTION, New Full Line Department Stores Designed by In-House Staff

Designer: Printemps
Paris, France

"Magasin de la Mode"

Before the renovation of the large, Printemps flagship store, every department in the eight-storey building had been concerned with home equipment. Since 1985, the basement, first and second levels have been devoted fully to women's fashions and are known as "Magasin de la Mode."

The rebirth of the store included a strategic repositioning of departments and a total rethinking of space utilization. The design had to combine the clients' long-established perception of this store, still expressed in the home equipment areas, with a renewal of the image for the women's fashion floors.

The newly renovated "Magasin de la Mode" provides a soft, feminine background for the superior quality women's fashions displayed. The decision was made to install the Lingerie World in the basement. A pink champagne atmosphere of charm and intimacy is created in a circular alley. A life-size bust, by the sculptor Coutelle, is complemented by round-cornered furniture.

Encountering Emotion in Fashion

On the store's first level, works of art and design details by Philippe Starck include profiled spaces, a floor of Carrara marble, a water-green arch of triumph, a metal-gray amphitheater and imposing swinging clocks hung at strategic crossways.

The second level is remodeled to strengthen the notion of space and aerated volumes. A 2.25-meter wide, circular alley, tiled with black granite, absorbs the light pouring from stucco ceilings. Large, artificially illuminated glass cupolas at the crossways and subtle chromatic manipulations enable a comprehensive understanding and viewing of fashion.

The new design is an expression of th company's commitment to be a partne in the process of creativity and to encourage, through total space utilization, a new mode of communication with customers—"to le them encounter emotion."

Project:	Printemps de la Mode
Location:	Paris, France
Client:	Au Printemps S.A. Paris, France
Design Firm:	Printemps Paris, France

INTERIOR DESIGN TEAM:

Planner:	Raymond Lajonie
Designer:	Bernard Collet
Decorator:	Raymond Lajonie
Job Captain:	Raymond Lajonie
Partner in Charge:	Philippe Vindry
President/Chairman:	Bruno Vallee
Consultant:	Philippe Starck (first floor only)
Photographer:	O. Mauffrey

The contrast between black and white is again used to enhance the merchandise effectively. The combining of opposites—the black table and black lingerie, juxtaposed with the light-colored mannequin and white floor—emphasizes the sensuality of the merchandise.

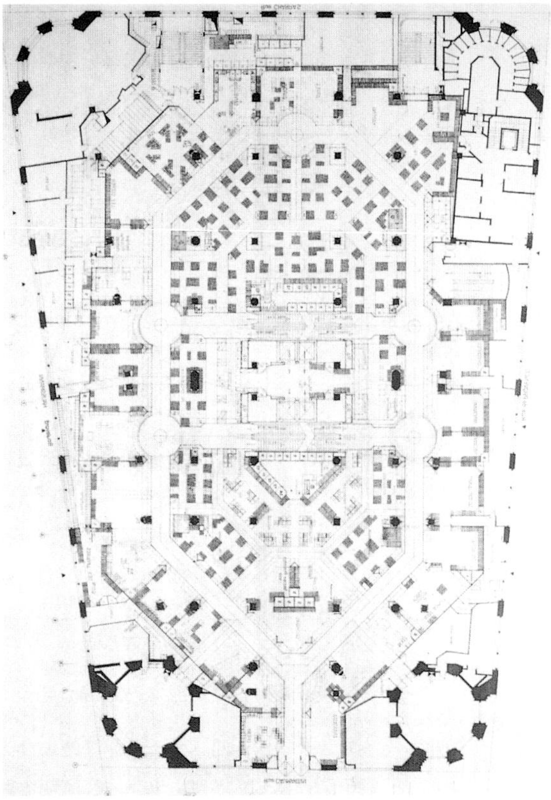

The store is filled with artwork that reflects the overall theme. This allows the customer to "encounter emotion" through the stunning and chic fashions available. Each section is distinguished by its own unique character and design.

Printemps
de la mode
Printemps
de la mode

Large glass cupolas are placed at some of the crossways. Black tiled floors absorb the light reflected off the white stucco ceiling.

The clean-lined Carrara marble archway looks deceivingly lightweight. The archway frames the focal point of the space—the jewelry.

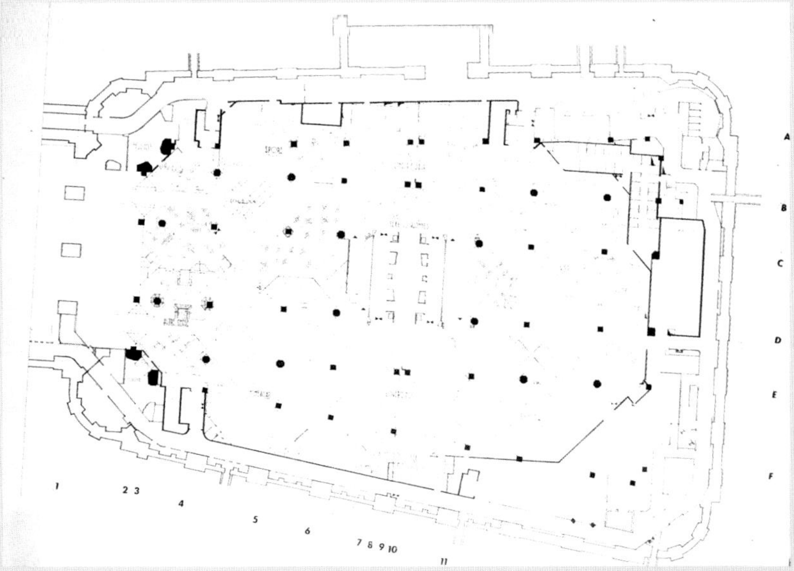

The simple, graduated tops of the display racks and the neutral black and white background color scheme allow the merchandise to capture the attention of the shopper.

discount
ROSY

The focal point of the pink champagne atmosphere is the octagonal skylight. Lighting concealed in the display units just above the floor level makes them appear to "float" on a layer of brightness and contributes to a feeling of airiness and lightweightedness in the spaces.

CHAPTER 5

Soft Goods Specialty Stores

Soft goods specialty stores usually contain a limited range of merchandise, such as fashion merchandise and accessories, linens, piece goods and draperies. The merchandise generally is geared towards upscale clientele, whose main concern is finding purchases quickly, rather than saving money.

Though each of the three stores featured here are designed with upscale customers in mind, the store structures and design themes are very different.

The detailed creation of a great country house environment in the POLO/Ralph Lauren Madison Avenue townhouse shop reflects the elegant lifestyle enjoyed by those for whom the merchandise is intended. The four levels of the shop are filled with an extensive range of merchandise, as well as with props, antiques, and accessories—such as model boats, straw hats, old photographs, fish trophies, and Persian rugs. These are carefully planned to make the customer feel at home in the Old World style of living depicted by the shop's setting. Extensive restoration of the Rhinelander Mansion, in which the shop is located, was conducted to make possible this one-of-a-kind store.

Each department is distinguished by a different character. The Men's Department, paneled in rich mahogany, is reminiscent of a classical English haberdashery. The Women's Department projects a lighter and airier ambiance via the light-colored walls and the soft lines of the upholstered furniture. The Home Furnishings level contains cozy, realistic settings that change seasonally.

Saks store designs usually make reference to local traditions. The Palm Springs store is no exception and reflects not only the glamour and elegance long associated with the city's wealthy lifestyle but complements the surrounding desert location as well. Three marbles—desert sand, clay and pale terra cotta—echo the desert and the elegant city.

The store itself is open and airy due to the octagonal arrangement of uplit vaulted ceilings that frame a larger two-storey skylit atrium. Fluted lines are carried through on columns and back walls and are etched into mirrors and glass, adding classical elements to the design.

Soft colors also are used at Green's. A periwinkle carpet and soft blue-gray ceiling run through all the departments. Other elements of color and form, however, distinguish individual departments and establish an eclectic design style with a touch of high-tech. In the Junior Department, a mauve pipe space frame containing lighting fixtures is suspended over a fashion model ramp. Ladies Sportswear and the Men's Sport and Dress Apparel Departments both have salmon-beige stepped valances over salmon-beige painted walls. White-on-white decor is used in the Children's Department, with eye-catching blue "Baby Teeth" signage.

All three stores succeed in projecting environments which appeal to the tastes and lifestyles of the desired clientele.

POLO/Ralph Lauren

New York, New York

Saks Fifth Avenue

Palm Springs, California

Green's

Middletown, New York

POLO/Ralph Lauren New York, New York

FIRST AWARD, Soft Goods Specialty Store, New or Renovated & Grand Prize

Designer: Naomi Leff and Associates
New York, New York

Preservation and Restoration of a Landmark

It was the intent of POLO/Ralph Lauren to create a retail environment which reflected the elegant lifestyle of the merchandise. POLO/Ralph Lauren is located in the Rhinelander Mansion, a National Registry building, built in 1889 on Madison Avenue. The adaptation of this building for a retail environment required a tremendous commitment to preserve the remaining outstanding interior ornamental details and to reconstruct the exterior of the building.

The base building, which had been blighted over the years, had to be extensively renovated. Life-safety and building code requirements had to be satisfied. The building systems and means of egress had to be integrated. So as not to disturb the existing ornamental plaster ceilings, the floors above were removed and the lighting and sprinklers were dropped in. Existing wood ceilings, where possible, were removed, restored and reinstalled. Layers of gypsum board were applied to existing wood joists to provide the required fire rating, and sprinklers were placed between the joists.

Because of the potentially high wattage per square foot required for retail use, a low-voltage lighting system was used wherever possible. Since the elaborate plaster ceilings were built against the building floor structure, the ductwork for the HVAC system could not be installed above those ceilings. Consequently, two machine rooms have been installed—one in the lower level and one in the roof hip—to eliminate as much vertical penetration as possible. An intricate and creative design was developed to run the ductwork behind the crowns of the fixture work.

Significant restoration of the existing architectural ornamentation has been done, including the casting and reconstruction of plaster details. Where mahogany wood paneling existed, it has been stripped of layers of paint and restained. Hand-carved ornamental and decorative features have been matched to the few existing architectural clues. Partitions have been designed to reestablish the scale and geometry of the ravaged interior. The planning issues have been used to recreate a residential scale to the space.

Elegance Combined with Accessibility

The store is planned, organized and designed to appeal to the customer and to enhance ease and accessibility of shopping. The first two floors are dedicated to the Men's Collection, with the addition of gift items. Using wood mahogany paneling, the Men's Collection reflects an English haberdashery. A hand-carved balustrade on the monumental paneled stair leading to the Second Floor is a major focal point.

The third floor is devoted to Women's Ready-to-Wear and Accessories. The lighter ambience contrasts with that of the lower levels. Separate areas are devoted to distinctive groups of merchandise, i.e., Collection, Roughwear, Activewear, Shoes.

The fourth floor contains Home Furnishings. The space is anchored by several lifestyle rooms which are designed seasonally as the New Home Furnishings Collections are introduced.

To date, sales have surpassed anticipated projections.

Shown is a display in the Men's Clothing section on the second floor.

Saks Fifth Avenue Palm Springs, California

HONORABLE MENTION, Soft Goods Specialty Store, New or Renovated

Designer: Hambrecht Terrell International
New York, New York

Skylit Atrium Hub of Octagon

Saks Fifth Avenue, a major American department store, is renowned, not only for its luxurious merchandise, but for its respect for store environments. In each Saks store there is a unique recognition of local tradition, whether it be the sophistication of a major metropolitan area or an ultracasual southwestern image.

In the latest Saks store, located in Palm Springs, the design reference is the glamour and elegance long associated with that city's wealthy lifestyle. In addition, lightness and clarity of color to complement the desert atmosphere are significant design factors. Finally, the store of 50,000 square feet has been planned to "feel" like a larger unit of 75,000 square feet.

An octagonal arrangement of uplit vaulted ceilings frames a larger two-storey skylight atrium that soars to 35 feet. The concentric plan allows for broad openings into each department with the highly desirable advantage of shallow depths.

Locale Reflected in Earth-Colored Marbles

Three marbles are used throughout the store to define the aisles: a desert sand, clay and pale terra-cotta. These complement the desert mood and are, in turn, the inspiration for faux marble walls and columns. The most dramatic of these are the tripartite columns of the atrium. Each portion of a column is composed of one of the faux marbles.

A secondary theme of fluted lines adds a classical element to the design. These lines appear on the columns, major back walls, and are etched into mirrors and glass screens to unify the shops.

The result is a carefully orchestrated plan, highly axial and formal in its scheme, blended with the soft earth colors of the desert—a combination so definitive of the city itself.

Project:	Saks Fifth Avenue
Location:	Palm Springs, California
Client:	Saks Fifth Avenue New York, New York
Design Firm:	Hambrecht Terrell International New York, New York

INTERIOR DESIGN TEAM:

Planner:	Art Kramberg
Designer:	Sue Sweeney
Decorator:	Debra M. Robusto
Job Captain:	George Hume
Project Manager:	John Czorny
Vice President:	John Czorny
President/Chairman:	James E. Terrell, Edward C. Hambrecht
Contractor:	B.K. General Contractors
Suppliers:	Bigelow (flooring), Lightolier (lighting)
Photographer:	Jack Boyd, Costa Mesa, California

One of the themes carried throughout the store is classical, fluted lines. In the Fine Jewelry Department, these lines appear on the columns. The two-storey atrium is capped by a skylight.

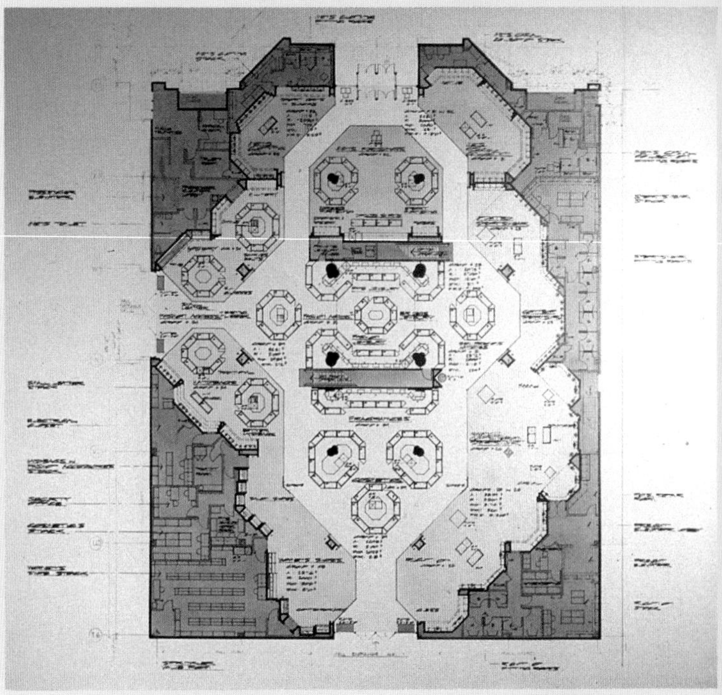

The concentric plan allows for broad entrées and shallow depths for each department. Faux marble columns and walls appear throughout the store.

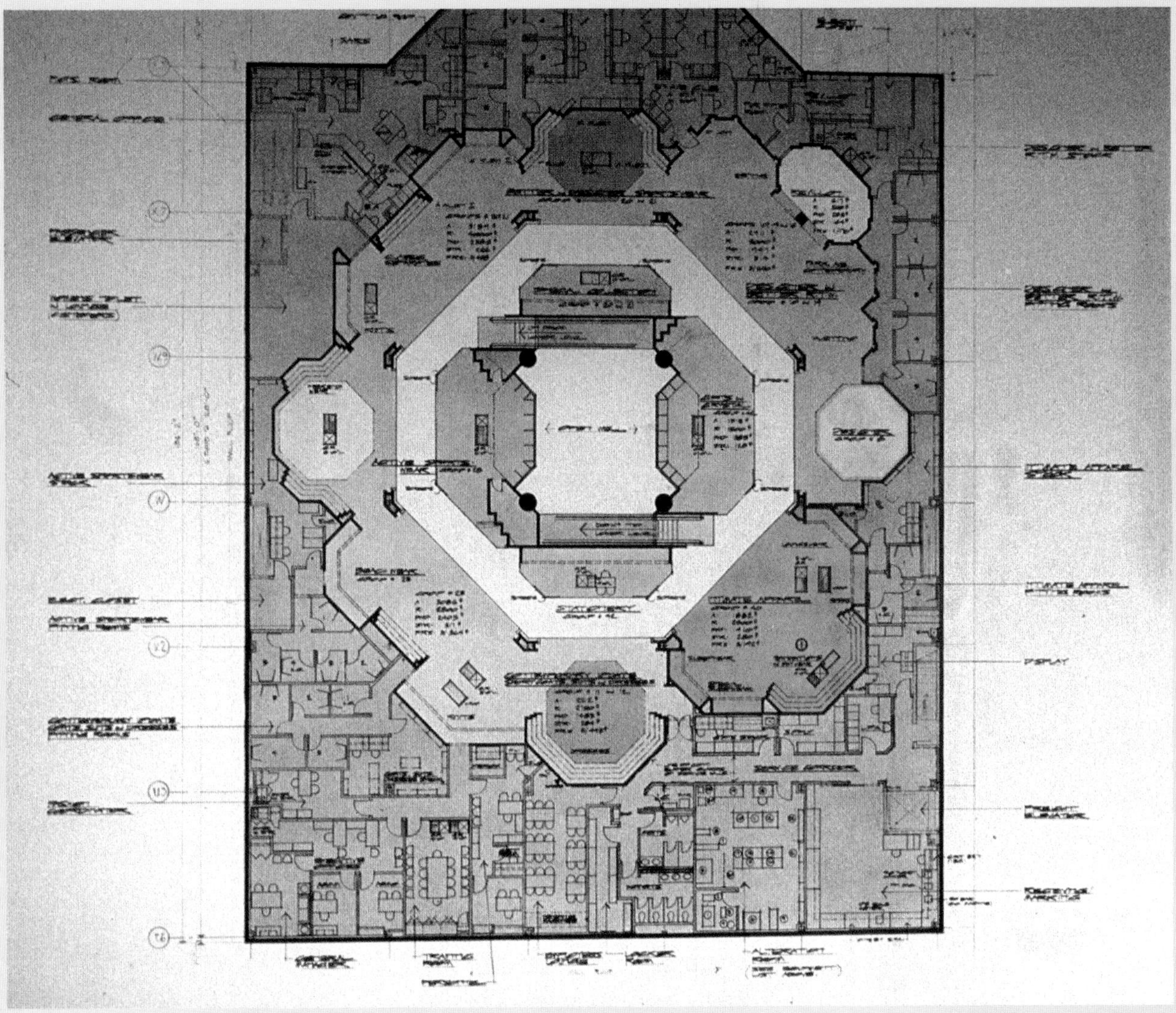

In Contemporary Sportswear, uplighting creates an open, spacious feeling. The octagonal arrangement of the vaulted ceilings frames the atrium.

Three shades of marble, seen here in Ladies' Ready-to-Wear, are used to define the aisles: desert sand, clay and pale terra-cotta.

In the Fragrance and Cosmetics area, the light colors have been chosen to complement the desert location of the store.

In the Ladies' Shoe Department, the fluted lines appear etched into glass.

In the Ladies' Shoe Department, the sculptured back wall of soft blue-gray is highlighted by a pure white neon script sign. White baker's racks and étagères are used to display merchandise.

Shoes

Green's Middletown, New York

HONORABLE MENTION, Soft Goods Specialty Store, New or Renovated

Designer: Design Team/Ruellan
New York, New York

Increase Sales through Replanning

Minor changes had been made through the years in Green's store design since it opened in 1971. But it neither looked the way it did when Raymond Loewy/William Snaith designed it, nor was it obtaining the best return on its space. Renovation was long overdue. The design team was required to replan and redesign the store to obtain the maximum results with a limited budget.

A productivity analysis was conducted which confirmed that eliminating the gift department and utilizing the space for certain higher productivity departments would increase the store's gross volume by over 40 percent in two years. Schematic plans were devised with improved customer traffic flow through the store. Stock rooms were eliminated as there is a large basement marking room with plenty of storage space. Finally, the store was reshaped to provide identifiable homes for all the departments and to open up spaces which had previously been hidden.

The design approach is eclectic, with touches of high-tech and post-modernism. The color palette is soft and seems almost monochromatic. Periwinkle gray carpet is used in all the departments. The off-white, vinyl tile aisle system has a diagonal border of 12-inch by 12-inch blue tiles alternating with white. The ceilings, also painted a soft blue-gray, seem to disappear except for the sparkle of the incandescent lights. The 4-foot by 4-foor fluorescent fixtures are glare-free due to the use of parabolic louvers.

The facade of the store has been changed from the Aztec geometry of the early 1970's to oak planking stained a soft gray. Inside the store, near the entrance, the large cosmetics showcase island separates the traffic flow.

Two large, backlit photomurals, promoting the two largest cosmetic resources carried in the store, face the showcase island and are part of small niches created by 8-foot high, white stepped partitions. These niches also contain major mannequin displays on the rear sides which introduce the Ladies Sportswear Department on the right of the main aisle, and Menswear on the left. Salmon-beige, stepped valances mounted on salmon-beige painted walls enhance both departments.

Between Men's Furnishings and Sportswear, the small shop for Men's Shoes is identified by 8-foot high, white stepped partitions and a white space frame suspended from the ceiling. Three-hundred watt tungsten flood lamps, clamped onto the space frame, are fitted with barn doors to eliminate glare and are used to illuminate the 8-foot high partitions. A mirror image of this shop occurs on the other side of the aisle between Petites and Ladies' Sportswear.

Another series of displays, stepped 8-foot high partitions and space framed shops are passed before reaching the black showcase island dedicated to jewelry and accessories. The island is silhouetted against two white 8-foot high walls containing fashion hosiery displays. Shops with green and white color schemes are devoted to handbags on the left and to scarves, belts and small leather goods on the right.

Fashion Model Ramp for Juniors

A mannequin placed on the steps of the fashion model ramp invites the shopper to participate in the next fashion show in the Junior Department. Special lighting for fashion shows is mounted on a mauve-pipe space frame which runs along the ramp to four circular fitting rooms at the rear of the island department. Fashionable merchandise adorns the model ramp on adjustable face-outs.

The Children's Department, identified by blue "Baby Teeth" signage, has white-on-white decor and merchandise grouped by age and sex. The Ladies' and Children's Shoe Department, with a sculptured, blue-gray back wall, is highlighted by a pure white, neon script sign. White baker's racks and étagères display the varied merchandise.

The Lingerie Department is adorned with an Art Deco two-step valance in two tones of peach, mounted over an off-white back wall. This is consistent with the feminine feeling which continues through Ladies' Dresses and Coats. Nestled discreetly in the corner of the Dress Department is a smart entrance foyer to what appears to be a private club.

Green's now has the store the quality of their merchandise and service deserves. Their customers agree.

Project: Green's
Location: Orange Plaza
Middletown, New York
Client: Donald Green
Design Firm: Design Team/Ruellan
New York, New York

INTERIOR DESIGN TEAM:

Designer/President: André Ruellan, F.I.S.P., A.S.I.D.
Contractors: Modern Woodcrafts (fixtures), Pittman Painting (painting), Harry F. Rotolo and Son (electrical), Walsh Floors (flooring)
Suppliers: J&J Industries (carpeting); Amtico Division of Biltrite (tile); Benjamin Moore (paint); Swivelier (display lights); Polyplastic Forms, Mid Hudson Neon (signage); Adelphia, Creative Dimensions, Gordon International, Shelby Williams Industries, Flex, Monel (furniture); Kee Klamp (space frames); Garcy Corporation (racks and fixture hardware); Laminart (plastic laminate); Wolf Gordon, Dazian Fabrics, Laue Wall coverings, Ametex (fabrics)

Eight-foot-high, stepped partitions, adorned with photomurals, separate the cosmetics section from the main aisle and the other departments.

Glare from the fluorescent lighting system has been eliminated through the use of 4-foot by 4-foot parabolic louvers. Periwinkle gray carpeting is used in all departments.

The perimeter of the Lingerie Department is accented by a peach-toned, two-step valance mounted over an off-white back wall.

Accessories and jewelry are housed in a black showcase island. Fashion hosiery is displayed on two 8-foot-high walls.

CHAPTER
6

Hard Goods Specialty Store

The characteristics of the hard goods store directly affect the store's layout and design. Since the customers' visits to these stores are usually infrequent, they would not be readily familiar with specific locations of the merchandise they seek nor with the services available. Consequently, the hard goods store should be designed to induce the shoppers' quick recognition of the kind and quality of store they are entering and the location of the types of merchandise available. Because the hard goods store generally appeals to a broader range of clientele than a soft goods store, the need for elaborate, limited-appeal ambience is reduced; the direct display of merchandise is more desirable.

Also, the layout of the store must allow for full and easy viewing of the merchandise. The design theme, in some cases, must also convey to the customer that the store maintains an expertise in its specialized field. Rather than feature superfluous decoration, an atmosphere of professionalism or high standards often can be conveyed thematically and through materials and furnishings.

Each of the stores featured in this chapter deals successfully with the characteristics of the hard goods environment. Interestingly, each of the stores embodies a different style to reflect the quality and nature of the products and services offered.

IPCO 'Super' Optical, which combines a testing area for eye examinations, a full-service laboratory and a sales area, had to project an atmosphere of competence, efficiency and professionalism. Clean, ordered lines and subtle colors are used in all three areas. The examination, fitting and laboratory areas are placed toward the back of the store, out of the mainstream of customer traffic, to increase privacy. The furnishings and lighting set the professional tone appropriate for the uses of these spaces.

Though the departments are separate, they are unified through consistent color schemes and design themes. For example, a grid-like module has been custom-designed to be used throughout the store as a display unit, as identifying signage and as a display of related photographic transparencies.

There are no unrelated displays or decorations that hinder the customer from perceiving exactly what the business and services of the store are. Contemporary-styled, curly maple sales islands are positioned at the front of the store for the shoppers' convenient viewing of eyewear. Straightforward neon signs at the perimeter of the store identify departments and services.

At Shreve's, the classical approach taken is reflected most strongly in the layout of the store. Showcase islands and tall, circular columns flank the main aisle.

The departments—china, jewelry and giftware—are separate, but are not formally divided by walls or partitions. The departments are visually linked through materials and furnishings—walnut cabinetry and mouldings, delicately patterned carpeting, and "window furniture" showcases. The conservative, elegant atmosphere convey to customers the awareness that they are in a quality shop that features superior merchandise.

At Crabtree & Evelyn, the array of varied merchandise—gourmet foods and European bath products—is unified by the English countryside theme carried through in the furnishings and materials—wood cabinetry, brass and glass accents—and embodied in the quaintly-decorated product packaging. Easily readable headers on the tops of the cabinets clearly announce to the shopper the type of products contained below. As in Shreve's, there are no obstacles or formal divisions between types of products. The major display is a variety of products charmingly arranged around a column that is visible from outside the entryway of the shop.

All three stores can accommodate heavy traffic flow. In all cases, the displays concentrate mainly on the products themselves and use materials and furnishings to decorate and to promote a particular style or atmosphere. Thorough knowledge and understanding of the products and services offered are the keys to creating the appropriate design for the small hard goods store.

IPCO 'Super' Optical

Lakewood, Colorado

Crabtree & Evelyn

Millburn, New Jersey

Shreve's

San Francisco, California

IPCO 'Super' Optical Lakewood, Colorado

FIRST AWARD, Hard Goods or Home Furnishings Specialty Store, New or Renovated

Designer: Planned Expansion Group, Inc.
White Plains, New York

Three Areas: Distinct but Unified

The client envisioned a "super" optical store of approximately 6,000 square feet which would combine a sales area, a testing area for eye exams and a full-service laboratory. An updated image and a more attractive and flexible display format were additional requirements.

A cohesive whole has been created of three areas with distinct personalities and needs: the theatrical drama of a retail space; the calm professionalism of a doctor's office; and the clinical order of a laboratory. These areas are unified through color and consistent design themes, but each is provided with an appropriate level of drama and exposure.

In the sales area, the center islands of curly maple with dramatically illuminated tents overhead and the perimeter fixtures finished in a soft gray laminate and washed in light appear to float against the dark ceiling, fascia and floor. This contrast is exploited to focus attention on the product.

The clean, ordered lines and subtle colors of the examination and fitting areas toward the back of the store are those of the sales area, but the furnishings and lighting set a very different tone. They establish a credible atmosphere of professionalism appropriate to the use of the space.

The offices and the laboratory at the rear of the store are concealed except where window grids visually integrate this area and reveal the functional organization of the lab.

Special Display Unit Developed for Sales Area

A display format has been developed for the sales area which can accommodate the display of glasses or accessories, identifying signage or display transparencies. The dimensions of a pair of glasses determined the size of the basic interchangeable module of the system. This rectangle is paired with another to form a square. Four of these squares comprise a display unit, each of which is backlit. The display units are integrated into the overall store design by their visual relationship to the black stripes and window grids used throughout.

Neon signs at the perimeter clearly identify the areas of the store and categories of frames. Signage noting subcategories and specific styles of frames is easily incorporated into each display.

The client's new image is forcefully established in this dramatic, yet practical, store. The new display format is adaptable to many and changing needs, the signage simplifies the task of the customer, and the areas of the store are seamlessly meshed while acknowledging their different natures.

Project:	IPCO 'Super' Optical
Location:	Lakewood, Ohio
Client:	Sterling Optical Woodbury, New York
Design Firm:	Planned Expansion Group, Inc. White Plains, New York

INTERIOR DESIGN TEAM:

Designer:	Robert W. Grzywacz, Director of Design
Project Managers:	Peter A. Cole, Design; Albert J. Krull, Implementation
Partner in Charge:	Kenneth D. Narva
President/Chairman:	Matthew E. Kroin, I.S.P.
Contractor:	Atmor Construction
Photographer:	Elliot Fine, New York, New York

The grid-like theme used in displays within the store is introduced at the entrance and frames eye-catching photos.

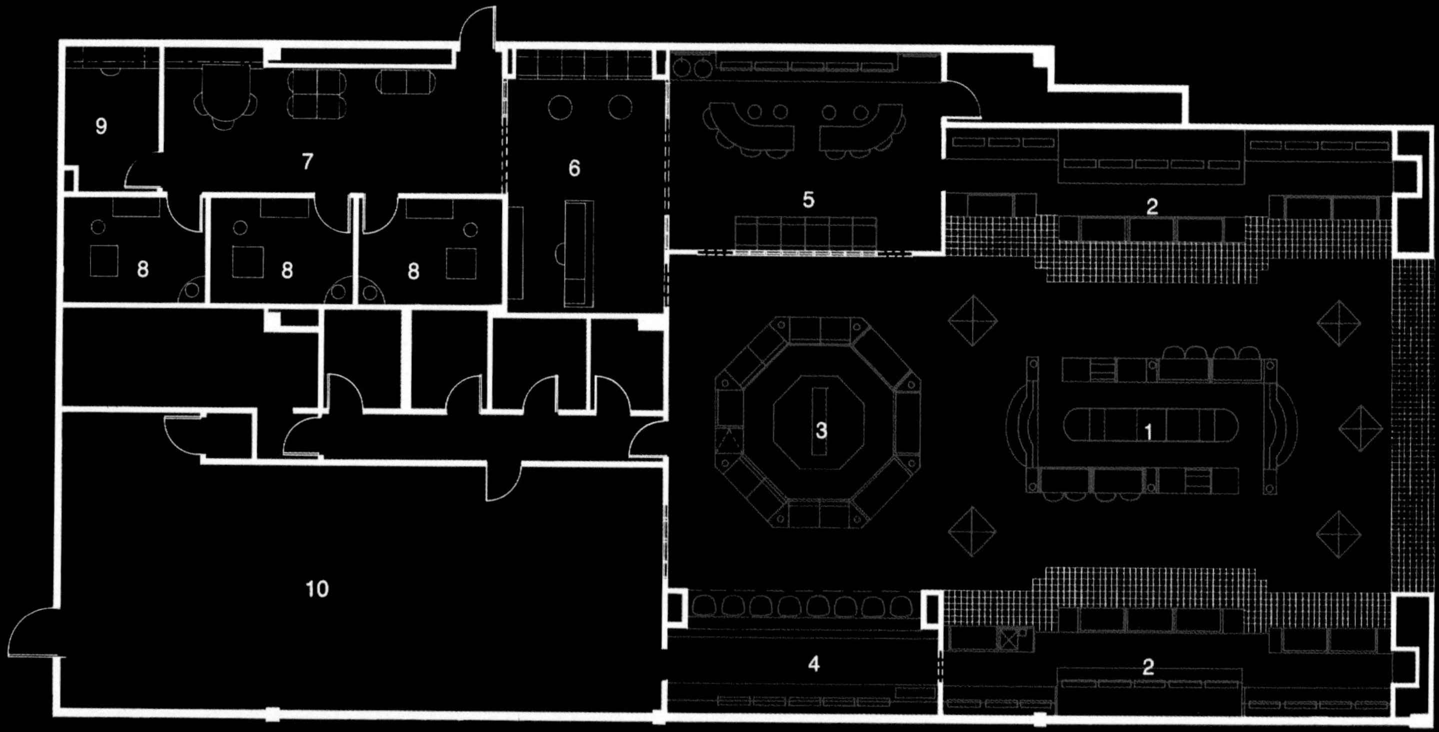
9
7
6
5
2
8
8
8
3
1
10
4
2

IPCO Super OPTICAL
HIS 'N' HERS
ELEGANT
Readers
HI-FLYERS

Each modular display is composed of four backlighted square units which can feature signage, products or transparencies. The window-grid design theme is used throughout the store.

SS PICK UP
ESSORIES
cases
STERL-AID
SPEK-AID
Replacement
deluxe cobra spec chain
LENS KLEENER
EYE CATCHERS
BARS

The fitting and adjustment area, adjacent to the lab at the back of the store, maintains a crisp, professional look aided by the subdued gray, white and black color scheme.

The examination area is set apart from the more hectic selling spaces. The area is uncluttered, with ample seating for those who need to wait and comfortable spacing between the examination stations.

Different types of merchandise and categories of eyeglass frames are identified by bold neon signs in areas lining the perimeter of the store.

Selling islands made of curly maple are illuminated from canopies above. The nondistracting dark ceiling and floor allow customers to direct their full attention to the merchandise.

Shreve's San Francisco, California

HONORABLE MENTION, Hard Goods or Home Furnishings Specialty Store, New or Renovated

Designer: The International Design Group Inc.
Toronto, Canada

Entrance Moved to Create Classical Layout

The original store had a major planning contradiction. Access from the corner, usually an ideal location, entered awkwardly at a 45 degree angle to the symmetrical layout of the whole building. The designers have repositioned the existing decorative bronze doors to follow a classical layout with showcases flanking the main aisle and a colonnade of marblized columns.

The walls are lined with polished walnut cases in tall, gracious proportions that are framed with rounded glass. The carpet is custom designed and provides a rich, decorative bed encircling all showcases and fixtures. Budget restrictions prevented carrying the classical detailing into ceiling beams and revising lighting in the ceiling.

The elegance of scale, size and detail of a turn-of-the-century store have been captured through the fine detailing and quality materials, which in turn reflect the high quality of the jewelry, china and giftware merchandise.

Full-View Storefront Windows

The building housing the Shreve store was one of the few to survive San Francisco's 1907 earthquake and, therefore, is an important historical landmark. The store's design had to enhance and to enrich the character of the existing exterior and interior.

Decorative metal canopies have been hung from the building over the windows to provide weather protection and shelter from sunlight for window displays. The window areas are completely open so that the interior of the store can be viewed from the street. The displays inside the shop are contained in sleek "window furniture" units.

Project:	Shreve's
Location:	San Francisco, California
Client:	Henry Birks (USA)
Design Firm:	The International Design Group Inc. Toronto, Ontario, Canada

INTERIOR DESIGN TEAM:

Designer:	Ronald J. Harris, I.S.P.
Job Captain:	Juan Esquijarosa, I.S.P.
Partner in Charge:	Ronald J. Harris, I.S.P.
President/Chairman:	Alan S. Fairbass, I.S.P.
Contractor:	F. Wiley Contracting Ltd.
Photographer:	Dennis Rider, Feature Four Ltd., Toronto, Ontario, Canada

A small office is enclosed by a polished-walnut frame fitted with rounded glass. Polished-walnut display cases also line the wall.

SHREVE & CO.

At one end of the store, next to the jewelry counters, large polished-wood topped vertical display cases house fine giftware.

Showcases and marblized columns with scroll-design capitals flank the main aisle A rich, intricately patterned carpet adds to the elegant ambience of the store.

The well-appointed office is beautifully wood paneled and illuminated by simple, incandescent downlights.

Due to budget limitations, the original fluorescent troffer lighting system has been retained.

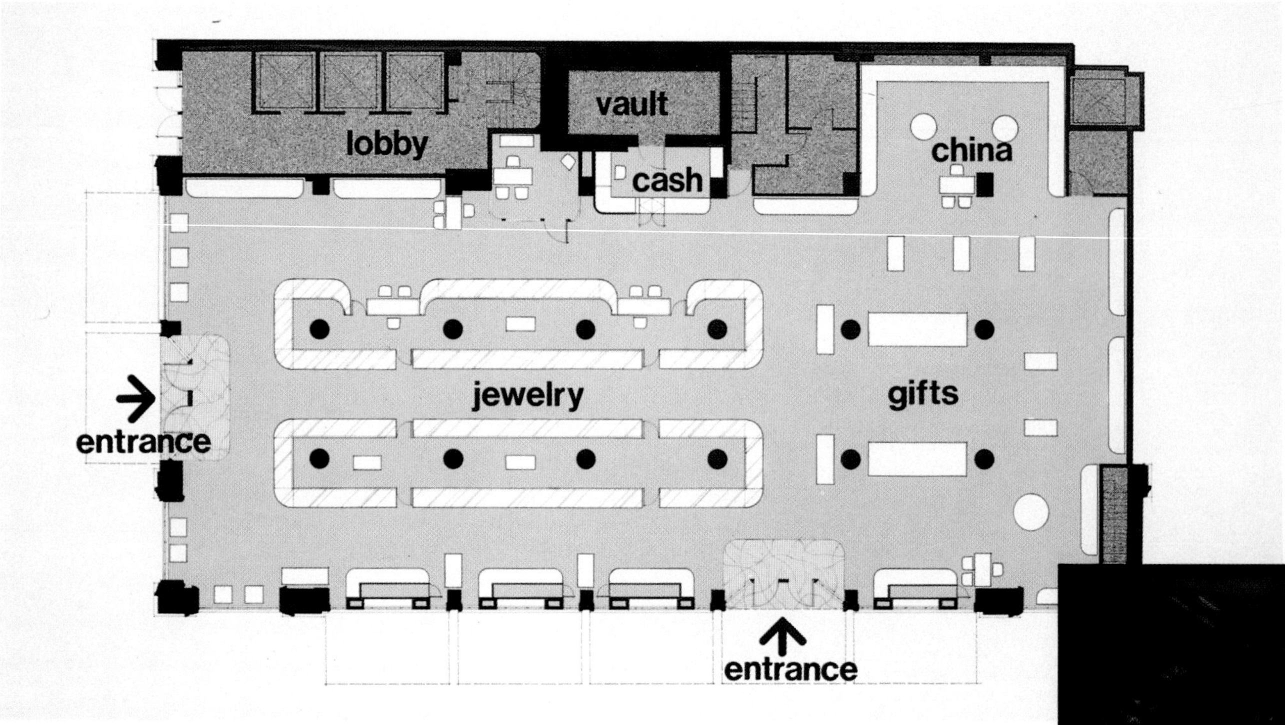
vault
lobby
china
cash
jewelry
gifts
entrance
entrance

A corner entrance has been removed and entryways placed on two sides to enable a classic, symmetrical layout to be established inside the store. The full glass front provides a complete view within.

Crabtree & Evelyn Millburn, New Jersey

HONORABLE MENTION, Hard Goods or Home Furnishings Specialty Store, New or Renovated

Designer: International Design Group (USA) Inc.
New York, New York

Quaint English-Countryside Image

Crabtree & Evelyn, in the Mall at Shorthills, is devoted to very specialized merchandise: a combination of high-end European bath products and gourmet foods. The designer's task was to combine the client's quaint English-countryside image with a design dramatic and eye-catching enough to compete in a suburban mall.

Customer appeal begins with the high and unusually-shaped storefront enhanced by full height glazing and a very articulated facade. Transom windows made of leaded glass panes are set over arched display windows that set the image and allow a full view into the store.

Inside the shop, a potentially troublesome structural column has been utilized by grouping around it graduated displays that draw the passerby's eyes into the store.

Lightboxes have been placed in the rear of the store to highlight translucent packaging in display cabinets. This also helps draw potential customers through the store.

Brass, Glass, and Custom Details Add Elegance

Traffic circulates freely around a central, marble-topped cash station, which also displays jarred potpourri. Walls are lined with dark wood cabinet display units. Shelving is installed at varying heights. Cabinets are backed in key locations with gray mirror. Cabinet headers clearly name the types of products displayed below.

The use of brass railing, glue-chip glass panels, old-fashioned brass track lights and custom bordered carpeting also add to the quaint, yet rich image desired by the client.

Project: Crabtree & Evelyn
Location: Millburn, New Jersey
Client: Crabtree & Evelyn, Ltd.
Design Firm: International Design Group (USA) Inc. New York, New York

INTERIOR DESIGN TEAM:

Designer: Matthew L. Tager
Partner in Charge: Keith Kovar, I.S.P.
Contractors: Intercity Construction (general), Custom Woodproducts, Inc. (cabinetry)
Photographer: Daniel Cohen, Hoboken, New Jersey

The awkwardly placed building column is used to advantage by surrounding it with a bountiful display that captures the character of the English countryside.

CRABTREE
&
EVELYN

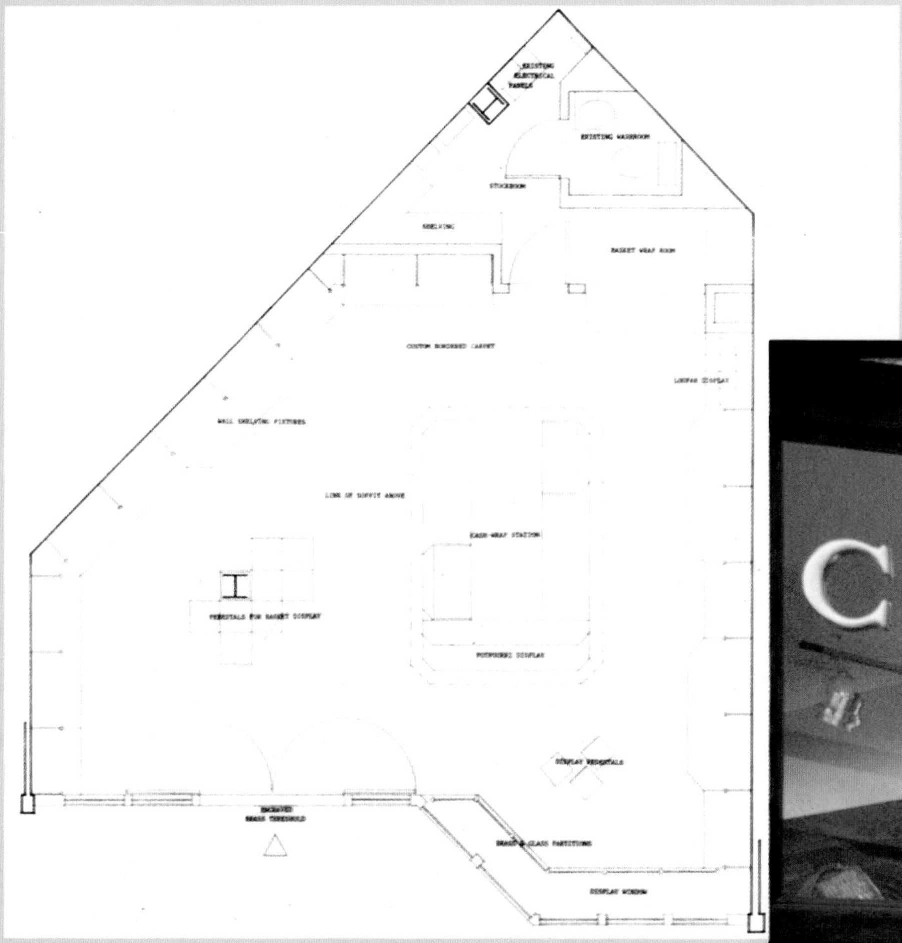
EXISTING ELECTRICAL PANELS
EXISTING WASHROOM
STOCKROOM
SHELVING
BASKET WRAP ROOM
CUSTOM BORDERED CARPET
WALL SHELVING FIXTURES
LINE OF SOFFIT ABOVE
CASH-WRAP STATION
PEDESTALS FOR BASKET DISPLAY
POTPOURRI DISPLAY
DISPLAY PEDESTALS
ENGRAVED BRASS THRESHOLD
BRASS & GLASS PARTITIONS
DISPLAY WINDOW

CRABTREE
&
EVELYN

The charm and appeal of the shop is evident to the customer even before entering. Old-world style transom windows, made of leaded glass panes, sit above arched display windows.

SETS
Crabtree & Evelyn
LONDON

Custom brass track lighting units and ornate sconces highlight the cabinet displays. Shelf height is varied to suit the size of the product.

FROM FRANCE

Key in projecting the quaint, old-fashioned quality of the products into the shop, is the careful attention to detail: the delicate border on the walls above the display cabinets, the solid dark wood with gleaming metal door knobs, the subtly patterned carpeting, the glass panels braced with shining brass rails.

The marble-topped cash register area is used for display also. The open space surrounding the counters is wide enough to allow free-flowing traffic circulation.

PRESERVES
TEAS & HONEYS
SPICES

Merchandise in translucent packaging stands on shelves in front of a backlighted panel. The bright panel and colorful bottles help attract customers to the back of the store.

CHAPTER 7

DEPARTMENT STORE RENOVATIONS: FLOOR OR DEPARTMENT

Motivations for renovating a department or floor are varied. A change in merchandise may necessitate an alteration in the setting. A refocusing of the store's direction or the type of customer to be targeted can require an updated image. Renovation can be cosmetic or involve major restructuring.

Two different approaches to renovations are included in this chapter. The redesign of Robinson's Men's Department, which is the first phase in the renovation of the entire store, relies on the existing classical architectural elements to establish a cohesiveness of design among the different merchandise areas within the department. Harrods Ltd. Perfumes, on the other hand, is not part of a total store renovation, and its futuristic style is achieved mainly through the choice of materials, colors and forms.

Robinson's Men's Department has the overall look of a classical haberdashery. Each section in the department, however, maintains an atmosphere that reflects the particular type of merchandise available. The materials used vary with the desired setting. For example, mahogany moldings and plain painted walls adorn the traditional men's area, ceramic tile and rubber are featured in the activewear area, and concrete stucco and steel piping with taut wire and crimson accents enliven the young men's area. The existing classical archways and vaulted ceiling visually unify the varied sections into one department.

At Harrods Ltd. Perfumes, the futuristic look is reflected in materials more than through existing architecture. Norwegian black granite heavily flecked with mica, stainless steel, automobile-finished surfaces, backlighted etched glass, mirrors, and wallcoverings made of mauve Thai silk blend to form a modern, sleek, but feminine and elegant background for the collection of superior-quality fragrances. Showcases designed with contrasting curves ease traffic flow, and soften the space.

Both stores' designs take into consideration the merchandise to be sold and the customer desired. Both departments add a freshness and liveliness to the stores, and project the image desired by the client.

Robinson's Men's Department

Los Angeles, California

Harrods Ltd.
Perfumes, Harrods Department Store

London, England

Robinson's Men's Department

Los Angeles, California

FIRST AWARD, Department Store Renovations: Floor or Department

Designer: Hambrecht Terrell International
New York, New York

Arches Bordering Rotunda Unify the Design

Robinson's original store in downtown Los Angeles had deteriorated over the decades. It was time to renovate the store completely. The total redesign is planned to take place in phases over several years. Currently completed is the first floor Men's Store.

The image projected is that of a classical haberdashery, a traditional men's store. The architectural focal point is a central rotunda with arches and columns around the circumference. The ceilings in the Men's Store are 20 feet high.

Each department is treated individually, but all are visually cohesive due to the series of arches and vaults which provide the customer with an impression of intrigue as he glances from one end of the store to the other.

Design Motifs Vary with Clothing Types

On the left side of the rotunda, the environments are formal and traditional. Ralph Lauren has a shop very much like his prototype on 72nd Street in New York. Slacks are in custom-designed units opposite the Lauren shop. The dress furnishings room is an oval, reflecting the formality and reserve of a London tailoring shop. The men's suit department also evokes classical themes and details.

On the right side of the rotunda is a more informal "dress down" world with a gymnasium-like arena for active clothing and a Japanese-inspired minimalist interior for young men's wear.

Appropriate materials are used in keeping with the distinct style of each area. For example, a herringbone inlaid wood floor and inset carpets serve as accents for the simply painted walls in the traditional men's area. Ceramic tile and rubber are used in the activewear environment. Concrete stucco and steel pipe with taut wires and crimson accents highlight the young men's area.

Each smaller environment reflects the particular type and image of products displayed, while projecting an overall strong and friendly design statement. The new design twists within the traditional framework of a men's haberdashery have resulted in an effective, exciting selling space.

Project: Robinson's Men's Department
Location: Los Angeles, California
Client: J.W. Robinson's
Los Angeles, California
Design Firm: Hambrecht Terrell International
New York, New York

INTERIOR DESIGN TEAM:

Planner: George Bonet
Designer: James E. Terrell, Fred George
Decorator: Debra M. Robusto
Job Captain: Guillermo Perrera
Project Manager: Dennis Morganelli
Partner in Charge: George Bonet
President/Chairman: James E. Terrell, Edward C. Hambrecht

Consultant: David A. Mintz (lighting)
Contractors: Standard Cabinet (cabinetry), W.A. Carroll (paint)
Suppliers: Barrett Hill, Laue Wallcovering, Knoll
Photographer: Jack Boyd, Costa Mesa, California

The Ralph Lauren shop, similar to the 72nd Street, New York City store, is tr tional and formal in layout and design.

The classical styling of the shop, suggested by the repetition of archways, is evident immediately upon entry into the Men's Department.

The central rotunda is the focal point of the department. Arches and columns line the circumference.

Light-colored walls and carpeting, and uplighting of the ceiling's center circle contribute to the airy, spacious feeling in the rotunda.

The ceilings are 20 feet high. Here, a vault echoes the classical, curved archways.

Classical themes and details are employed in the suit area. The rounded corners of the dark ceiling reinforce the archway theme.

Harrods Ltd. Perfumes

Harrods Department Store, London, England

HONORABLE MENTION, Department Store Renovations: Floor or Department

Designer: WalkerGroup/CNI
New York, New York

Futuristic Styling and High-Quality Materials

A 6,000-square-foot enclave at Harrods Department Store has been transformed into a bold, theatrical and elegant showcase for fine fragrances from all over the world. The design of the new perfume hall is based on a contemporary, dramatic design concept distinguished by forms, colors and materials of high quality and enduring beauty.

Instead of traditional vernacular of white and black, a high-style futuristic design has been developed. The advanced contemporary look is dominated by the use of Norwegian black granite, heavily flecked with mica, in floors, walls and showcase islands. The rich surfaces and material are enhanced by elements of stainless steel, automobile-finish metallic surfaces and back lighted etched glass and mirrors. They are softened by upholstered wall coverings of irridescent mauve Thai silk. All the elements reflect the highest standards of detailing.

Contrasting Curves Feminize

To create a browsing traffic flow, and to soften and feminize the space, a motif of contrasting, curved forms has been introduced everywhere: the selling islands, the sculptured ceilings, the rounded detailing of columns and perimeter selling fixtures and the shape of cash register stands. Sculptural glass panels in the Lalique manner elegantly divide one alcove from another.

It is axiomatic in contemporary store design that sophisticated lighting techniques are fundamental in achieving exciting and dramatic selling space. The designers used this principle and developed the lighting around advanced types of small aperture, high-intensity, low-voltage incandescent downlights. These fixtures, placed within th curved ceiling vaults to reflect the curved edges of all showcases, create a dazzling galactic pattern.

The total integration of architectural spatial designs with merchandise presentation techniques, result in a sumptuous and striking Perfume Hall.

Project: Harrods Ltd. Perfumes
Location: Harrods Department Store
London, England
Client: Harrods Ltd.
London, England
Design Firm: WalkerGroup/CNI
New York, New York

INTERIOR DESIGN TEAM:

Project Manager: Verinder Masson
Partner in Charge: Robert Herbert
President/Chairman: Lawrence Israel, F.I.S.P.
Contractor: Davies Shopfitters

Suppliers: Dupont, Ian Well (wallcoverings), October Co. (showcases)
Photographer: Chorley Hyman & Rose, Visual Aids Service, London, England

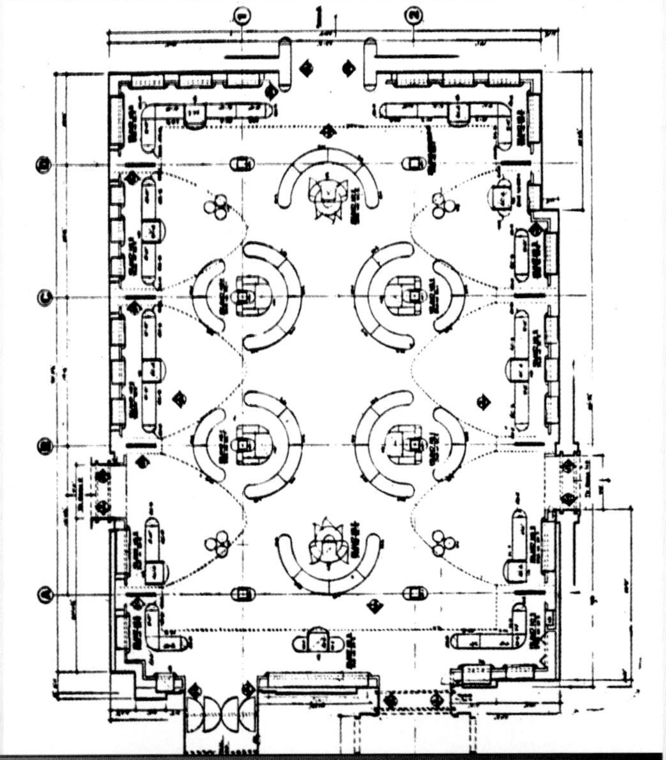

It is the attention to detail and rich materials that make the Perfume Hall particularly striking and elegant. Graceful female figures are etched into the vertical glass panels.

The gentle curves of the selling islands feminize the space and help ease traffic flow. The extreme contrasts in color—from the light ceiling and bright, illuminated columns to the dark floor and showcase trim—create a futuristic look.

The ceiling is studded star-like with recessed low-voltage, high-intensity incandescent downlights which illuminate the showcases. The Norwegian black granite, flecked with mica, dominates the floor, walls and showcase islands.

Curved archways reinforce the rounded showcases. The wallcoverings are made of soft, mauve Thai silk.

CHAPTER 8

SUPERMARKETS / CONVENIENCE STORES AND MASS MERCHANDISERS

A wide variety of products are stocked in supermarkets, convenience stores, and mass merchandise stores. Since these stores are generally self-service and do not have salespeople available to promote the products, display and presentation methods become critical in bringing merchandise to the attention of the customer. Due to the large quantity of products, displays are mostly functional, and many consist of ordered arrangements of the products themselves.

The customer's ease in locating merchandise is of primary importance. This necessitates the use of signage that is clear and easily understood, while contributing to the design theme of the store. Because the customer's visits to a supermarket are usually regular and frequent, the atmosphere should be made as comfortable as possible.

At Insalaco's Supermarket, attention is directed to the products by bathing them in illumination set at higher levels than the lighting in the aisles. Lamps are baffled or recessed to eliminate glare and to increase shopper comfort. The overall neutral coloring of the store also allows the customer's attention to be drawn to the colorfully packaged merchandise.

The lowered, coffered ceiling in the checkout area creates a sense of intimacy. Ceramic tiles decorated with energetic patterns and vertical breaks visually reduce the vast expanse of the space. Signage plays a major role in establishing the friendly, personal atmosphere at Insalaco's. Flowing script clearly identifies the departments, while smaller print subtitles add a touch of humor, such as in "Custom Cuts—Leave It to Cleaver."

The designers for Janovic Plaza created an effective, organized environment for the very broad range of decorative home improvement products available. A grid structure, which first appears in the storefront and displays a collage of products, is repeated within the store to define areas and departments and to act as a display device.

Customer comfort is taken into consideration also. Quick sale items are placed in open, loft-like, unfinished spaces. Items requiring more thought are grouped in smaller, intimate residential-scale settings which are defined by canopy-like structures suspended within the main loft space.

In spite of the large quantity of products, both stores have created quality environments which combine the functional and the practical aspects of the shopping experience with pleasing aesthetics and customer comfort.

Insalaco's Supermarket
West Pittston, Pennsylvania

Janovic Plaza
New York, New York

Insalaco's Supermarket

West Pittston, Pennsylvania

FIRST AWARD, Supermarkets/Convenience Stores and Mass Merchandisers

Designer: Off The Wall Company
Sellersville, Pennsylvania

Sophisticated Yet Friendly

Insalaco's Supermarkets have a reputation for honesty, friendliness and caring that can only be earned by years of good service and community concern. When planning their newest store, the Insalaco's wanted a unique, upscaled atmosphere while maintaining the friendly environment for which they are known. The well-planned fixture layout, specialized lighting, signage and finishes blend to create an attractive store with that "personal touch."

A large produce department at the entry is balanced by service departments located in the far corner that draw the customer through the entire store. Valances, which enclose the refrigerated cases along the store's perimeters, produce a custom look and eliminate possible clutter on case tops.

Product impact is enhanced and energy is saved through lower general lighting levels and higher lighting levels on the merchandise. Produce is illuminated by fluorescent fixtures with incandescent spots to add dimension and to enhance color. Pendant lights humanize the general atmosphere while directing special attention to the service meats and ice cream cases. Soffits are gently washed with fluorescent perimeter lighting that creates vertical interest and subtly defines traffic patterns. Valance lighting is used to highlight the grocery aisles. Through the entire store, lamps are baffled or recessed to eliminate glare.

Signage and Finishes Reflect Image

Signage helps establish the friendly atmosphere. As customers enter the store, backlighted produce signs embody the Insalaco theme: sophisticated yet friendly. A lovely flowing script allows for clear departmental identification. Smaller print subtitles add a touch of humor to each department. For example, the service meat department is identified with a "Custom Cuts" sign, and the smaller print reads, "Leave it to Cleaver!"

The overall store is neutral in color in order to allow customers' attention to be drawn to the merchandise. Clean, strong colors are used in small amounts to add punch.

Sophistication and casualness are carefully balanced in the finishes through the store. This is most evident in the combination of casual wood planking with a formal moulding on the valances. Grids are used to unify the design. Color reversal and material changes add interest and aid departmental identification.

The checkout area faces a 90-foot solid wall that was a special challenge. Here, friendliness is especially important. Ceramic tile with an energetic pattern and vertical breaks reduce the vast expanse. The lowered, coffered ceiling creates intimacy and overhead excitement which define this area. The tile pattern is repeated down the grocery aisles to add interest at floor level and to provide a cohesive visual theme throughout the store.

This fast track job was completed with a minimum of probems, because it was a team effort in which the owners, designers and contractors worked together toward a specific goal. The result is a good-looking, energy-efficient supermarket that reflects the Insalacos' concern for their customers. Three or more Insalaco's Supermarkets in the planning stages show how well the customers' reception and increased sales have been to this new store design.

Project:	Insalaco's West Pittston
Location:	West Pittston, Pennsylvania
Client:	Insalaco's Supermarkets Pittston, Pennsylvania
Design Firm:	Off The Wall Company Sellersville, Pennsylvania

INTERIOR DESIGN TEAM:

Designer:	Linda Anderson
Project Manager:	Sharon Jaffe
Partner in Charge:	Barbra Barker
President/Chairman:	Barbra Barker

Contractors:	Off The Wall Company (signage), American Refrigeration (refrigeration units)
Photographer:	Bob Hahn

The neutral tones of the floor, walls, ceiling and display cases allow the customer's attention to be drawn to the brightly-colored merchandise and signage. Backlighting adds dimension to the wall-mounted produce signs.

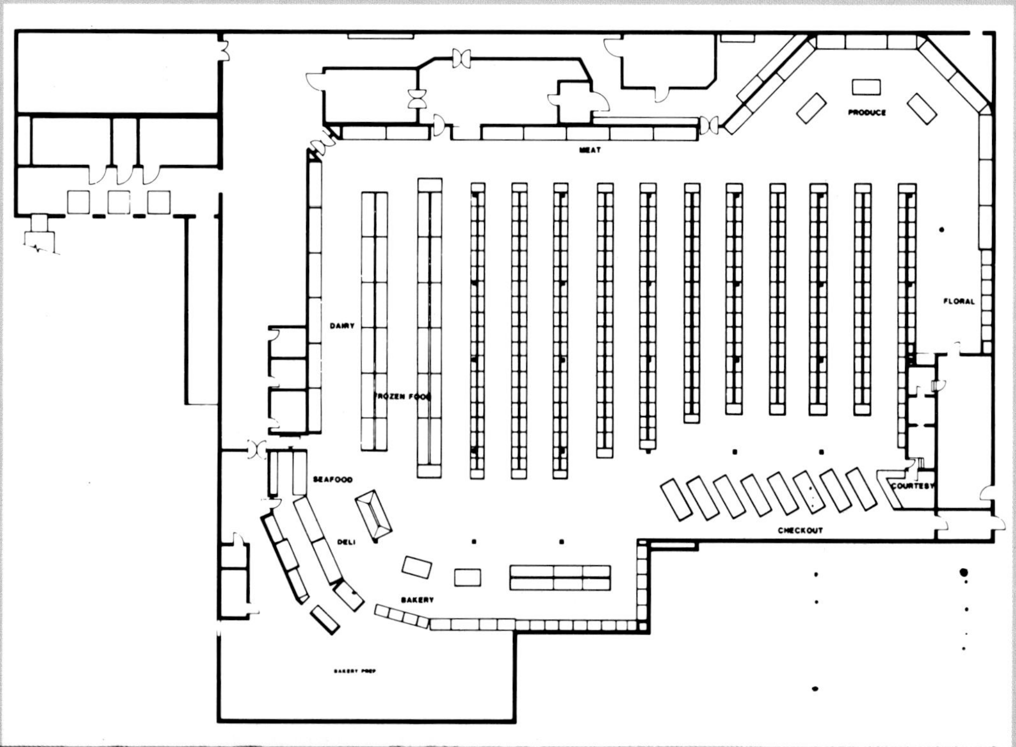

The customers' attention is directed toward the merchandise through the use of varied lighting levels: lower levels for general areas and higher levels for products. Here, ceiling-recessed downlights focus on the islands. Surrounding aisles are slightly subdued.

The colorful signs are easy to read, and the humor incorporated into them enhances the informal, friendly atmosphere the client desires. Note, for example, the circular, green and white "Frozen Food on the Rocks" signs.

The vast, 90-foot wall near the checkout counters is shortened visually by ceramic tile that displays a pattern with distinct, vertical breaks. The lowered, coffered ceiling creates a sense of intimacy and interest.

Janovic Plaza New York, New York

HONORABLE MENTION, Supermarkets/Convenience Stores and Mass Merchandisers

Designer: James D'Auria Associates, PC, Architects
New York, New York

An Organized Multi-Product Environment

Janovic Plaza is located on a busy avenue in New York City's Chelsea District. This area is experiencing rejuvenation, as inhabitants buy and renovate older buildings for residential use. The store occupies the ground floor of a 20-storey apartment building complex. The leased area is 7,000 square feet with a 15-foot slab-to-slab height.

An effective, organized merchandising environment had to be created for the very broad range of decorative home improvement products that includes paints and painting aides, stains, plaster, vinyl, floor and tile adhesive, wall paper, window treatments, fabrics and a complete bath shop.

Though budget limitations precluded a new storefront, the interior side of the existing glass configuration is enhanced through the use of an open, three-dimensional grid-like vertical display unit that allows a collage of products to be shown in a clear, orderly manner. The grid structure is repeated within the store to establish and to define areas and departments, as well as to act as a display device.

The T-shaped retail space is organized around two perimeter circulation spines that lead from the front of the store to the rear. Along these aisles, between the bays of merchandise, point of purchase displays have been developed for visual reinforcement and impact. These bays along the perimeter also incorporate, unobtrusively, the irregularly-placed building columns. Circulation spines and axes are further defined by suspended display platforms that both terminate the vista and announce the department.

Quick Sale and 'Pensive' Purchase Integrated

The space includes a series of clearly defined areas, each dedicated to the display and merchandising of a specific product. The custom paint shop (a Janovic trademark) is positioned close to the entry for immediate customer recognition. This is followed by stock paints, stain applications and other quick sale items that require ample space for both product and stock. At the leg of the "T" are the departments for wall paper, fabric, window treatments and bath accessories, items which require customer thought and concentration before purchase.

Quick sale items, such as the stock paints, are placed in open, loft-like, unfinished spaces. Items requiring more thought before purchase are grouped in smaller, intimate, residential-scale settings. These areas for custom paint, wall paper, window treatments and shower curtains are defined by a series of canopy-like structures suspended within the main loft space.

Materials and finishes were selected and developed in keeping with the overall design concept. The concrete floor is epoxy-painted, using passes of three colors over a ground color. Each color was applied with a customized roller developed by the designers.

Because the ceiling and its pipe and valve system had to remain accessible for maintenance, it is exposed, and painted a neutral color to avoid distracting the customers. Shelving and floor fixtures are stained particle board, occasionally faced with plastic laminate on wearing surfaces. Rubber bumpers are placed along all bases for protection and design continuity. Canopies, which serve as product enclosures as well as surfacing for the uplighting from the illumination system, are fabricated from lightweight perforated metal panels.

The materials used reinforce the design intent to integrate the dichotomy between the raw and the finished, the active and the passive, and the quick sale and the pensive purchase.

Project: Janovic Plaza
Location: New York, New York
Client: Janovic Plaza
New York, New York
Design Firm: James D'Auria Associates, P.C., Architects
New York, New York

INTERIOR DESIGN TEAM:

Design Team: James D'Auria, John James, Sherrie Zwail
Associate in Charge: John James
President/Chairman: James D'Auria
Consultant: Jack Green Associates (mechanical/electrical)
Contractor: F.J. Sciame Construction Co., Inc.
Photographer: Nathaniel Lieberman

Items requiring consideration and thought before purchase are set apart under canopy-like structures made from lightweight perforated and corrugated metal panels. Customers can compare products and plan color schemes seated comfortably at the table and chairs.

Striking and easily read yellow lettering announces the name of the store. Since the storefront could not be changed, a specially-designed, versatile, grid-like display unit has been installed and features a collage of products.

The Custom Paint Shop is a trademark of Janovic Plaza and is situated at the front of the store. Uplights are used to illuminate its canopy-covered cove.

CUSTOM MIXED COLORS

Although the piping from building systems is exposed on the ceiling, it is painted a neutral color to render it nondistracting to customers. Pendant-mounted fluorescent fixtures illuminate the aisles and merchandise.

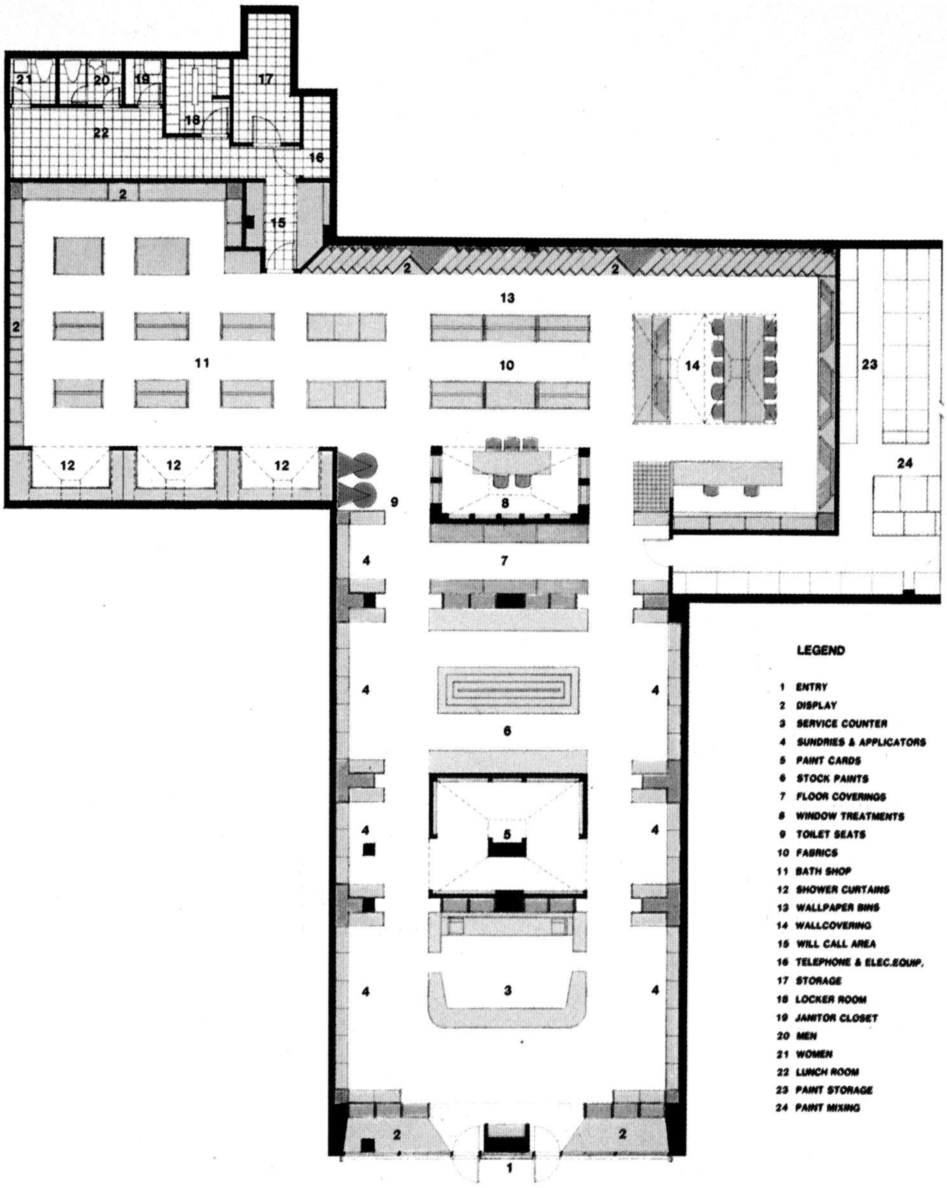
LEGEND
1 ENTRY
2 DISPLAY
3 SERVICE COUNTER
4 SUNDRIES & APPLICATORS
5 PAINT CARDS
6 STOCK PAINTS
7 FLOOR COVERINGS
8 WINDOW TREATMENTS
9 TOILET SEATS
10 FABRICS
11 BATH SHOP
12 SHOWER CURTAINS
13 WALLPAPER BINS
14 WALLCOVERING
15 WILL CALL AREA
16 TELEPHONE & ELEC.EQUIP.
17 STORAGE
18 LOCKER ROOM
19 JANITOR CLOSET
20 MEN
21 WOMEN
22 LUNCH ROOM
23 PAINT STORAGE
24 PAINT MIXING

CHAPTER 9

Small Soft Goods Stores

The creation of an "image" is particularly important for the small, soft goods store. The image serves several purposes: it attracts customers, helps customers identify easily the type and quality of the merchandise and helps improve sales by differentiating the merchandise and service offered from those of larger or department stores, and other, similar soft goods shops.

Images are formed in conjunction with the consideration of several influencing factors, including the location of the store, its size and the nature of the merchandise. Images are embodied in a cohesive blending of the logo, furnishings, displays, materials, and merchandising tools. The small size and shape of the store can often inspire the development of ingenious displays and merchandising techniques that reflect the desired image.

Three images which relate to merchandise in three different ways are featured in this chapter: a contemporary, quality store-styling, designed to reflect those same qualities found in the merchandise; an environment which incorporates merchandising tools that relate to the use of products; and fixture designs and layout which encourage the coordination of the varied products available and multiple sales.

The tailored, quality appearance of Tommy Hilfiger's is created through the use of superior materials, such as bleached oak and monochrcmatic granite floor tile, which form clean-lined storage/display areas. Binning contributes to the maintenance of the well-ordered appearance and makes maximum use of the small space. The backlit plexiglass skylight enables the confined area to look and feel more spacious and airy. The contemporary styling of the store appeals to the young, upscale customer desired, and directly reflects the inherent attributes of simple, yet superior detailed styling found in the clothing line.

Imaginative and eye-catching merchandising techniques developed especially for The Weather Store strikingly remind the customers of when the products are to be used. A *trompe l'oeil* sky overhead reacts to the sounds of a thundering rainstorm. The customer is safe, of course, from showers inside the cozy, country-house atmosphere of the small shop. The colorful merchandise is displayed in a variety of racks and stands that make maximum use of the limited space. At the checkout counter, the customer is greeted by a large window frame through which can be viewed an appropriate outdoor scene.

Small, clever details—such as the four seasons graphic outside the shop, and the blackboard behind the storefront window that announces the day's weather to passersby—immerse the customer in the "weather" atmosphere and promote the buying of the products which are used only occasionally. The sounds of the thunderstorm and corresponding lighting effects succeed in luring passersby into the shop to experience the audiovisual "show" while browsing through merchandise.

Colorlume, the computerized merchandising tool developed specifically for Casual Corner, serves a dual purpose. It is an attractive, modern colorful display that enhances the appearance of the shop. It is also an effective way to aid customers in coordinating colors as they choose the components of ensembles. This second aspect reinforces the "wardrobing" approach which is the key to the store's presentation and the basis for multiple sales. Versatile, custom-designed fixtures aid in organizing the merchandise, which is particularly important in a store where customers seek to mix and match several pieces of clothing. The fashionable, up-to-date image projected in the Casual Corner flagship store can be transmitted to other Casual Corner shops through the unique, white and copper fixtures and the computerized Colorlume display.

As demonstrated by the stores included in this chapter, there is no one way to produce a successful image. The image can be subtle or all-encompassing; reflective of the product itself or how it will be used; conveyed through innovative merchandising tools, or through simple-styled materials and furnishings. The small soft goods store can offer a large, exciting and interesting challenge to any design team.

Tommy Hilfiger

New York, New York

The Weather Store

New York, New York

Casual Corner Flagship Store

New York, New York

Tommy Hilfiger New York, New York

FIRST AWARD, Small Soft Goods Store under 6,000 Square Feet

Designer: Robert Young Associates, Inc.
Alexandria, Virginia

Tailored, Detailed, Quality Appearance

In planning the new Tommy Hilfiger store, the design team strove to achieve a tailored, detailed, quality appearance that would reflect the clothing designer's and manufacturer's concern for those same qualities in the merchandise. A simple, straightforward approach has been taken that produces a becoming visual impact as well.

The interior volume is used to its greatest potential and all visual barriers have been eliminated. Through the full-height glass storefront/entryway, the passerby is allowed a complete view of the store's clean-lined interior and neatly-stacked menswear. Binning is used for folded merchandise to maximize capacity and to maintain a sense of order.

Though the finishes are monochromatic, a sense of warmth is created by the bleached oak fixtures and flooring. Decoration in the store is simple and occurs only in the gleam of a minimum of polished brass accents and in the monochromatic granite tile floor border and wall treatment. Other finishes include painted gypsum board and ceiling, and a complementary-colored plastic laminate back in each bin.

Skylight Is Focal Point

Lighting is used as a key design element as well as to clearly highlight merchandise. The focal point of the store is the backlighted, plexiglass skylight, which lends an air of spaciousness and openness to the small, enclosed space. Recessed downlights and fixtures mounted on the inside rim of the skylight provide comfortable, glare-free illumination for the merchandise.

Project:	Tommy Hilfiger
Location:	New York, New York
Client:	Murjani International, Ltd.
Design Firm:	Robert Young Associates, Inc. Alexandria, Virginia

INTERIOR DESIGN TEAM:

Planner:	Woody Mosby
Designer:	Michael Wilkins
Job Captain:	Tom Ryan
Project Manager:	Woody Mosby
Partner in Charge:	Robert C. Young
President/Chairman:	Robert C. Young
Consultants:	William Weber Assoc., M.E.P., Douglas Baker (lighting)
Contractor:	Nikon Construction
Suppliers:	Granitello Marble, Putnam Rolling Ladders, Capri Lighting
Photographer:	Elliot Fine, New York, New York

A complete view of the merchandise in the small shop is visible through the full-length glass front.

TOMMY HILFIGER

Binning maximizes the use of the space. A mirrored wall adds to the illusion of spaciousness. Recessed downlights, fixtures mounted on the rim of the skylight and the skylight itself provide adequate and comfortable illumination of the merchandise.

REGISTRATION # 324
CATEGORY H
CODE 324

The focal point of the shop is the backlit skylight which is made of plexiglass and creates a more spacious, airy atmosphere in the small space.

The design is simple and straightforward. There are no visual barriers to obstruct viewing the merchandise. A soft, monochromatic coloring is achieved through the use of bleached oak fixtures and flooring, and the complementary granite tile floor border.

The Weather Store New York, New York

HONORABLE MENTION, Small Soft Goods Store

Designer: Joshua Burdick Associates
New York, New York

A Country House Motif

The Weather Store is a new retail venture initiated by the owners of an umbrella manufacturing company. Their concept is to sell umbrellas and related weather gear under one "sky" (roof). The store occupies a small, leased space in the South Street Seaport shopping center and focuses on the direct application of the merchandise.

The interior of the store embodies the atmosphere of a cozy country house in its slate floor and rough wood siding and ceiling. While paying for their purchases, customers are even treated to a pleasant view of the "outdoors." Behind the cashier's counter, in the back wall of the shop, is a 4-foot by 8-foot lightbox displaying a realistic picture depicting a scene of the appropriate season. The lightbox sits behind window framing to create the illusion for the customer of looking outdoors at a colorful and pleasant scenic view.

Since the space already had a predetermined shape, the designers strove to use every square inch to produce a maximum of product display in a variety of ways. For example, wearable gear is displayed along the left wall and on freestanding wooden racks in the center of the store; umbrellas are lined up neatly in vertical display stands.

Special Effects: Thunder and Lightning

The focal point of the shop is the skylight, which contains a *trompe l'oeil* rendering of a blue sky with white clouds. The fluorescent lights in the skylight blink and shudder in synchronization with the snap and rumble of lightning and thunder sound effects. Small window frames on the sides of the shop also look out on *trompe l'oeil* outdoor scenes, which mimic the reactions of the main skylight to the changing "weather."

The audiovisual show takes place every eight minutes and succeeds in attracting prospective customers who see the flashing skylight as they pass by the shop, stroll in to enjoy the sound and light experience, then browse through the merchandise.

Project:	The Weather Store
Location:	South Street Seaport New York, New York
Client:	American Umbrella
Design Firm:	Joshua Burdick Associates New York, New York

INTERIOR DESIGN TEAM:

Planner:	April Lee
Designer:	Mark Moody
Job Captain:	Kuei-Lin Tsai
Associate in Charge:	Umit Tambil
President/Chairman:	Joshua Burdick
Consultants:	Tech Sounds, I. Kotosky
Contractors:	H. Dym General Contracting, Interstate Store Fixture
Suppliers:	Stewart Technical Corp., Decrolite, Weyherhauser
Photographer:	Michael LeGrand

Clever details, such as the blackboard in the window that announces the day's forecast, help immerse the customer in the world of weather. The bursts of color from weather gear and accessories add liveliness and further interest in the small area.

The Weather Store
The Weather Store

The Weather Store
Monday
84° at South
Street Seaport
67% Humidity
The Weather Store
The Weather Store

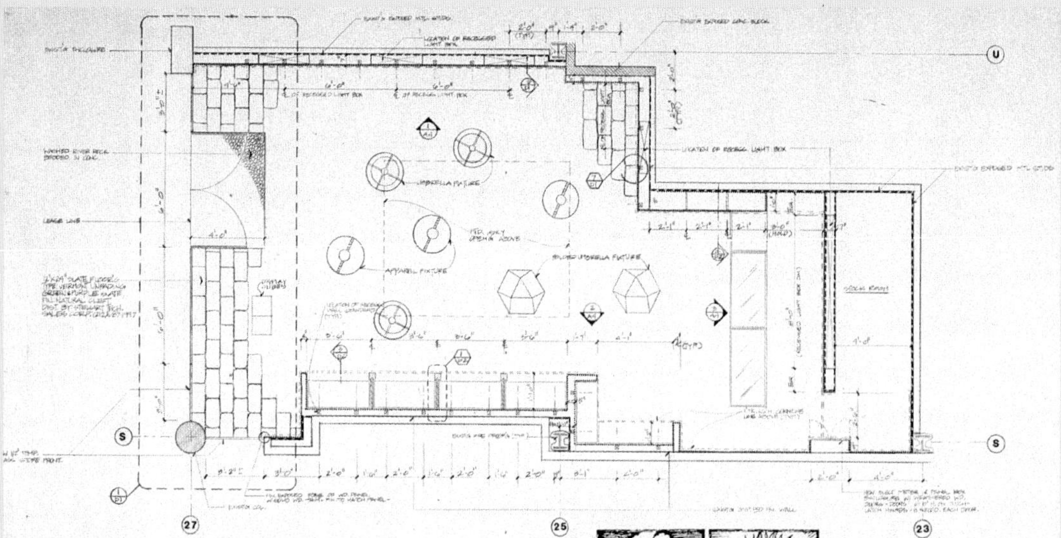

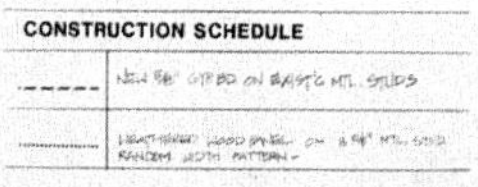

The Weather Store

GRAPHIC DESIGN

An outdoor scene can be viewed through the large wooden window frame by customers as they pay for the merchandise they've selected. The merchandise is stored and interestingly displayed in a variety of ways: on wooden racks, on vertical stands, in cubbyholes.

THE
TimesBOOKS

The slate floor and wood walls and ceiling create the look of a country home. The *trompe l'oeil* sky in the shop's center is the focal point of the attention-getting audiovisual thunder and lightning "weather show."

EXIT

Casual Corner Flagship Store

New York, New York

HONORABLE MENTION, Small Soft Goods Store under 6,000 Square Feet

Designer: Robert P. Gersin Associates, Inc.
New York, New York

"Wardrobing" Approach Is Key to Presentation

At the Casual Corner in Rockefeller Center, a new identity and design has been established that will be carried through other Casual Corner shops across the country. The store had to be designed to:

- compete more effectively for prime locations in malls
- respond to changing customer demographics and needs
- improve the store's image as a fashion authority for both customers and mall developers
- differentiate the store from department stores and other specialty shops
- increase sales volume.

The store logo's newly-selected typeface, stacked and screen-printed in white on transparent, edge-lit plexiglass, provides an appropriate signature for the new store design.

Casual Corner was the first store to use the "wardrobing" approach. This has been made the core of the store presentation. The customer can walk into the store, assemble an outfit for any occasion and choose all the accessories needed to complete it. The store plan groups similar types of merchandise together. Unique, flexible display fixtures are used to direct customer flow and to identify merchandise reflecting three different lifestyles: wear-to-work, casual and special occasion. The customer can quickly and easily see and select merchandise.

The eight versatile, custom-designed store fixtures are finished in high-gloss white and polished copper. These display fixtures are proprietary symbols for Casual Corner. The feature display module, a dramatic pivoting fixture, is used to shape the central space and provides the major merchandising statement in the store.

Colorlume—Computerized Merchandising Tool

A unique merchandising tool, Colorlume, has been introduced at this flagship store. Colorlume is embodied in a curved, floor-to-ceiling wall, dotted with colored circles, that wraps around the fitting room area. Through computer controls operated by employees, the range of colors within the wall's circles, the speed with which the colors change and the color intensity can be programmed to create a variety of effects. The intent is to reinforce the changing and seasonal combinations of colors reflected in the merchandise and displays.

Other architectural features include: a dramatic staircase and bridge to the mezzanine level, a two-storey copper cube which clads the elevator and a formed ceiling over the career-wear.

Lighting units are concentrated on the merchandise, highlight featured displays and create interesting contrasts between ambient light levels and the merchandise.

The functional and attractive design of this new flagship store eases product selection for the customer and the making of multiple sales for the staff.

Project:	Casual Corner Flagship Store
Location:	Rockefeller Center New York, New York
Client:	Casual Corner
Design Firm:	Robert P. Gersin Associates, Inc. New York, New York

INTERIOR DESIGN TEAM:

Planner:	Ingrid G. Caruso
Designers:	Sam Blay, Robin Tolud, Scott Bolestridge, Ralph Ehinger, Etienne Ma, Mike Beitler
Project Manager:	Ingrid G. Caruso
Associate in Charge:	Ingrid G. Caruso
Design Director/ President:	Robert P. Gersin
Consultants:	CHA Design, Inc., NYC (lighting), William Plachy (program)
Contractor:	L. Epstein & Sons (general)
Suppliers:	Parkway Wire Frame Corp., Garcy Corp., Metal by Dimensions, Eastern Wire (custom fixtures and hardware); Capri Lighting, High Tec Applications (lighting); Spanjer Brothers (signage); Lees Carpets, Permagrain (flooring); HEWI, Inc. (hardware); Nevamar Corp. (metal laminate); Hadley Exhibits, Inc., Litelab Corporation (colorlume)
Photographer:	Michael Datoli Photography

The custom-designed store fixtures contribute to the smooth functioning and ordered appearance of the store. A formed ceiling has been dropped over the ground floor Wear-to-Work area.

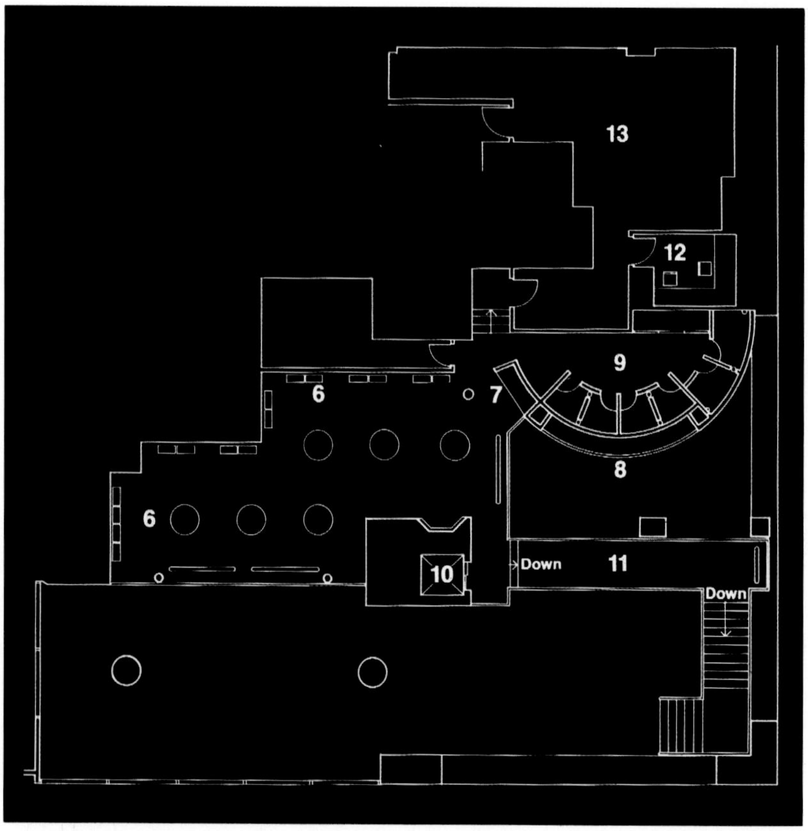
13
12
9
6
7
8
6
10
Down
11
Down

The Colorlume wall reaches to the ceiling of the mezzanine level. Recessed incandescent units create dramatic plays of light and shadow.

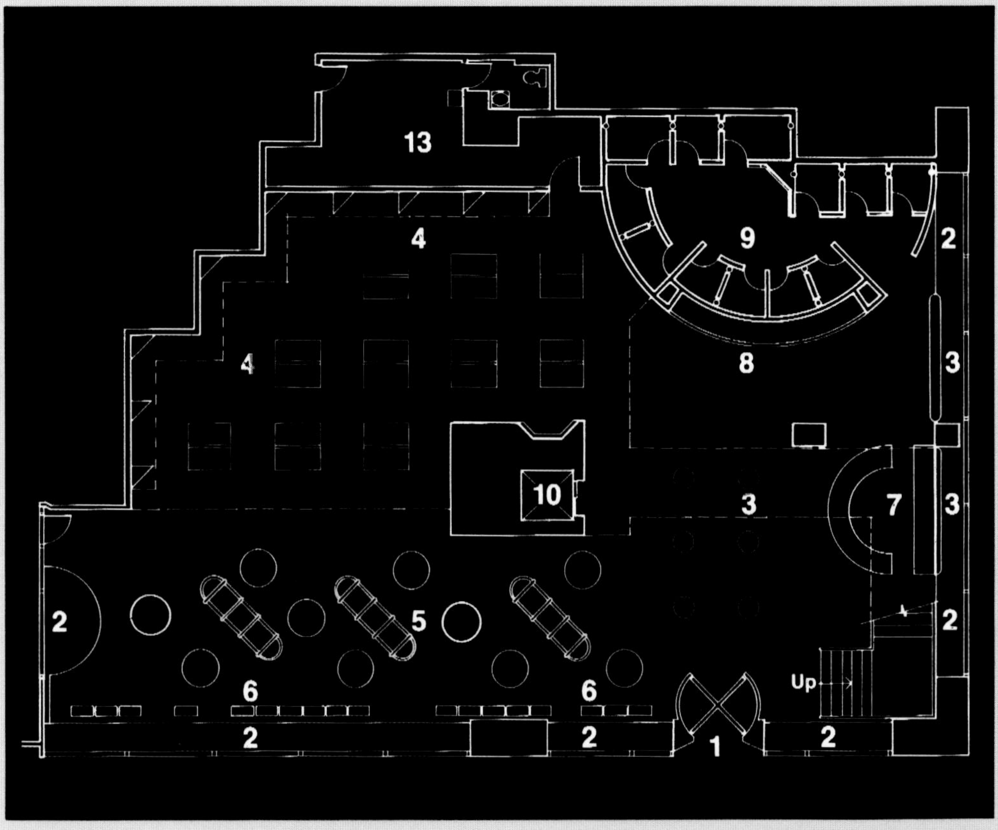

Striking architectural features include the copper-clad elevator cube, and the white staircase and bridge leading to the mezzanine level.

CHAPTER 10

SMALL HARD GOODS STORE

The limited area and classes of merchandise available in a small hard goods store make it especially important to avoid wasting valuable space. Even displays should be functional as well as decorative. The layout of the store is particularly significant in promoting efficiency and accessibility to merchandise and services.

All three stores in this chapter deal successfully with the considerations mentioned. Each store presented reflects a different type of service and merchandise.

At "Look" Hair Design, the reception desk is designed to serve as the shop's control point. Customers seated in the waiting area at the front of the shop, as well as the stylists at their workstations in the center and rear of the shop, can be viewed clearly from the desk. Glass-enclosed units that display products and accessories available are mounted along one wall in the waiting and workstation areas and are compact enough to allow complete freedom of movement through the aisle.

The long, narrow shop looks larger than it is due to the light, monochromatic floor, walls and ceiling and to the freestanding, angled mirrors at the workstations. The use of heavy-duty tile makes the shop easy to care for and virtually maintenance-free.

Efficiency and merchandise accessibility are primary concerns in Henry's Convenience Shop. The double entrance enables the store to be accessible and visible from all angles in the lobby of the building. Flexible wall presentation areas contain multiple levels of merchandise. A heightened sense of depth and space is created through the placement of the central counter in counterpoint with the curved wall. These concave and convex forms provide easy access to merchandise and ease traffic flow.

Before B & L Patisserie was designed, time and motion studies were conducted at the original location to provide the designers with insights into how the sales people work and how the traffic flows. The products gain maximum visibility displayed in simple, glass-walled cases and on angled wall-recessed shelves. The romantic touches which give the shop its unique character do not clutter or take up much valuable space—*trompe l'oeil* walls, small lichen trees placed in the out-of-the-way cash register area and Bacchus wall sconces mounted above the tables for two.

All three shops provide maximum efficiency and product visibility. Each also employs proven techniques to enlarge visually the limited spaces—light colors, counterpointed curves, mirrors and elimination of clutter.

"Look" Hair Design
New York, New York

Henry's (Convenience Shop)
San Francisco, California

B & L Patisserie
Los Angeles, California

"Look" Hair Design New York, New York

FIRST AWARD, Small Hard Goods Store
Designer: UMIT and Company
Rego Park, New York

Fresh, Striking Monochromaticity

The open salon concept of "Look" Hair Design in New York City fulfills four basic design criteria: functionality, practicality, and ease of circulation and maintenance. The striking monochromaticity is created through the use of tile on the floor and walls, cleanly defined with black grouting. The ceiling is composed of 2-foot by 4-foot acoustical ceiling panels designed to project 12-inch and continuous grout line looks. The crisp, light space appears larger than it is. The heavy-duty tile insures years of maintenance-free environment.

Because of the narrowness of the salon, the waiting area is located near the reception desk in the front of the shop. Four brightly colored chairs draw the attention of passersby to the store from outside. The control point of the store is the reception desk. From the desk both the entrance and the five styling stations can be viewed.

Easily accessible, wall-mounted display units are installed in the waiting area and behind the styling stations. The units display special hair products, jewelry and accessories.

Uncluttered, Spacious-Looking Styling Stations

The uncluttered styling area layout allows the operators freedom of movement. Freestanding mirrors placed at an angle add to the impression of spaciousness, and allow the customers to view television monitors while their hair is being styled. Though there are only two monitors, the positioning of the mirrors enables a monitor to be viewed at each of the five styling stations. A caddy tower positioned next to each mirror holds appliances and equipment needed by the stylists.

Towards the back of the shop, behind the styling stations, are two black marble shampoo bowls raised with vanity cabinets for easy access. A back wash system allows the assistant to reach all sides of the head. Behind these bowls, back-lighted, sandblasted panels display the super-graphics of the salon. The large, vibrant red logo can be seen from outside the shop.

All mechanical systems are neatly hidden in a room located behind the glass panels. There is a convenient coffee bar with a sliding door recessed into the wall next to the shampoo area.

The fresh look of the salon is enhanced by dimmer-controlled low-voltage lighting. All fixtures are finished with plastic laminate. At the cash register, a sandblasted glass top is supported with metal tubing. Display units are covered with lockable plexiglass. Freestanding mirrors are finished with brushed aluminum laminate.

Project:	"Look" Hair Design
Location:	New York, New York
Client:	Hendrika Tambil
Design Firm:	UMIT and Company Rego Park, New York

INTERIOR DESIGN TEAM:

President:	Umit Tambil, I.S.P.
Contractors:	American Concord, Inc. (general), Beacon Cabinets, Inc. (fixturing)
Suppliers:	Decrolite (lighting), Kruger (chairs), Tilerama (tile)
Photographer:	Michael LeGrand

Staff seated at the reception desk has a clear view of both the entry/waiting area in front and the styling stations in back. At the styling stations, the mirrors are angled so customers can watch the television monitors while having their hair styled.

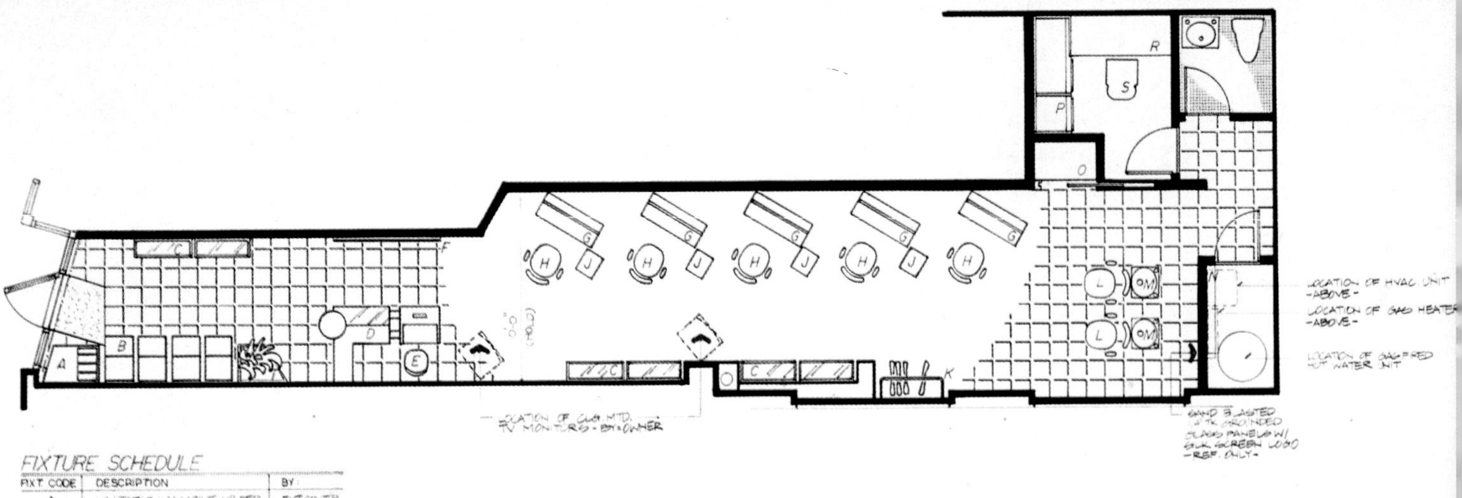

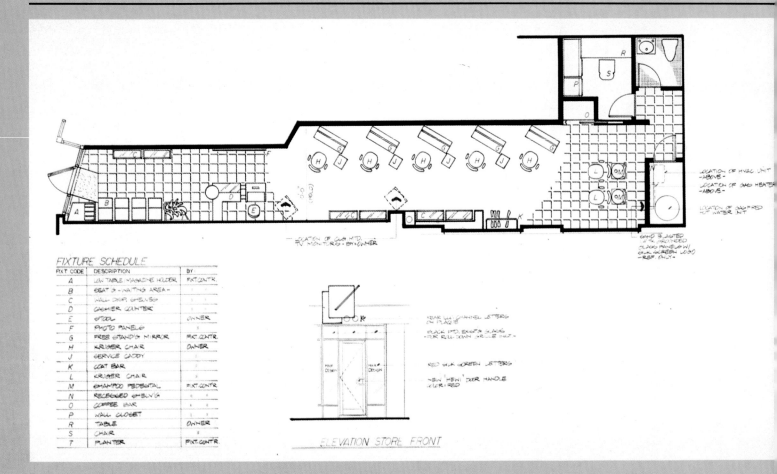

FIXTURE SCHEDULE

FIXT. CODE	DESCRIPTION	BY
A	LOW TABLE/MAGAZINE HOLDER	FIXT.CONTR.
B	SEAT'G -WAITING AREA-	" "
C	WALL DISP. SHELVES	" "
D	CASHIER COUNTER	" "
E	STOOL	OWNER
F	PHOTO PANELS	"
G	FREE STAND'G MIRROR	FIXT.CONTR.
H	KRUGER CHAIR	OWNER
J	SERVICE CADDY	"
K	COAT BAR	"
L	KRUGER CHAIR	"
M	SHAMPOO PEDESTAL	FIXT.CONTR.
N	RECESSED SHELV'G	" "
O	COFFEE BAR	" "
P	WALL CLOSET	" "
R	TABLE	OWNER
S	CHAIR	"
T	PLANTER	FIXT.CONTR.

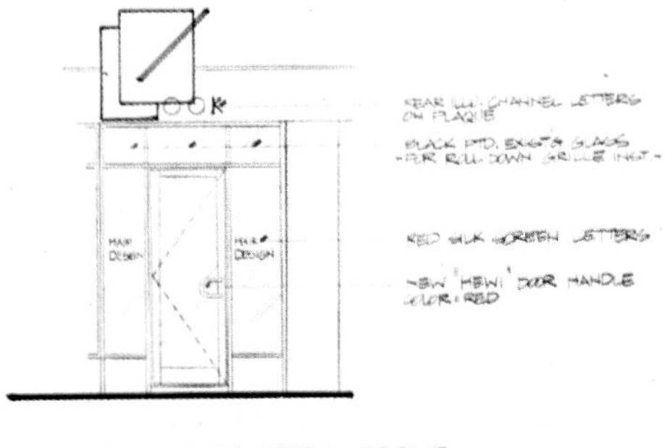

ELEVATION STORE FRONT

Both the brightly-colored chairs in the front of the store and the vibrant red logo at the rear of the store stand out against the monochromatic background provided by the walls, floor and ceiling.

The uncluttered styling stations include white cabinets next to the mirrors which contain all the appliances and equipment the stylists need. The wide aisle insures the stylists freedom of movement.

Display cases along the wall contain available hair products. A recessed downlighting system provides high-quality illumination.

Henry's San Francisco, California

HONORABLE MENTION, Small Hard Goods Store under 6,000 Square Feet

Designer: Planning and Design Concepts
San Francisco, California

Classical Facade Inspires Old World Ambience

The convenience shop is set within the luxurious, marbled lobby of a new bank building which incorporates the historically-preserved, classical facade of the original building with a modern atriummed glass tower. The marbles sense of history and elegance became the stepping stone for the traditional approach to the design of Henry's.

The primary requirements for the shop were: a double entry to allow easy visibility and access from the lobby; maximum, flexible wall presentation areas for merchandise; a securable, humidity-controlled cabinet; display refrigeration for food and drink; and a defined cash wrap/service counter. These requirements have been fulfilled within a very limited budget.

The Key Is Curves in Counterpoint

The central counter of the 11-foot by 17-foot shop is curved to maximize usable space and to soften the hard lines of the area. A heightened sense of depth and space is created because the counter is set in counterpoint with the curved side wall. The concave and convex forms provide easy access to merchandise and aid traffic flow. To ensure wide visibility of merchandise, the counter has a two-tiered presentation section at the bottom and a three-tiered presentation section at the top. The three-tiered, stepped configuration has curved, clear plexiglass lips which are imbedded into the millwork. The merchandise is highlighted by low-voltage spotlights which are built into the overhead storage area.

The side wall cabinets are individual modular units fastened together, with internal fluorescent lighting and adjustable shelving. The wood panel ceiling is suspended and hangs free of the perimeter walls, except for bracing. This aids the linear air diffusers in circulating fresh air.

All millwork was shop fabricated. Careful attention to detailing was maintained throughout. The curvilinear design and selection of materials—dark wood, brass, marble—combine an old world, traditional ambience, with modern convenience shopping.

Project: Henry's (Convenience Shop)
Location: Citicorp Building
San Francisco, California
Client: Henry Greenspan, David Thompson
Design Firm: Planning and Design Concepts
San Francisco, California

INTERIOR DESIGN TEAM:

Planner: Stewart Wyler
Designers: Stewart Wyler, Peter McCormick
Decorator: Peter McCormick
Job Captain: Stewart Wyler
Project Manager: Stewart Wyler
Partner in Charge: Stewart Wyler
Consultant: W.A. DiGiacomo & Associates (H.V.A.C.)
Contractors: George Wright (general), Alan Jones (millwork)
Suppliers: Innovative Ceiling Systems (ceiling), Halo Lighting (lighting)
Photographer: Douglas Salin, San Francisco, California

Lighting is integrated unobtrusively into a wood-finished canopy that mimics the circular central counter below.

HENRY'S
Amount Purchased
25
Trident
Trident
Trident
Trident
Trident

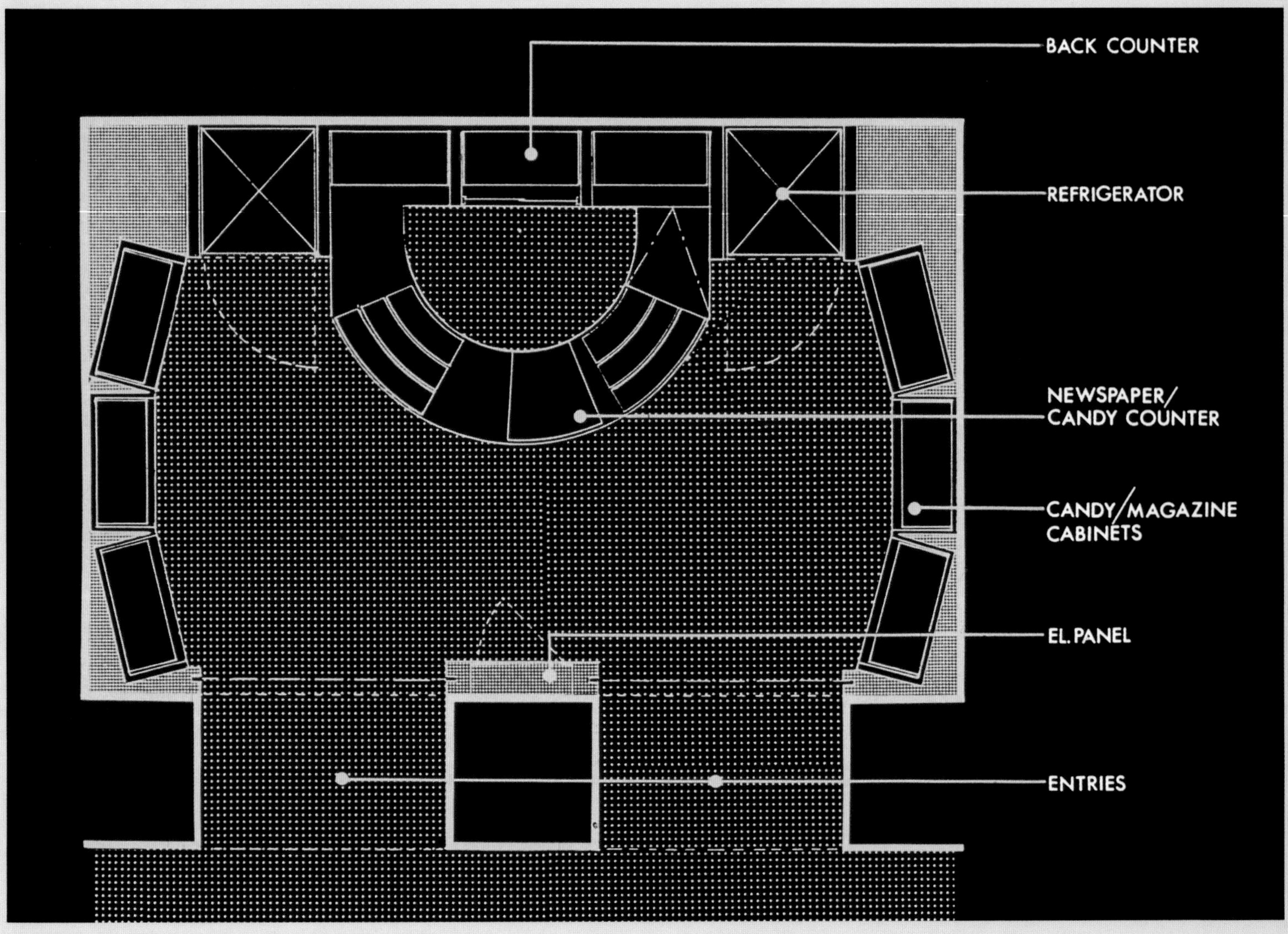

Rich, golden lettering simply announces "Henry's." The marbled lobby inspired the traditional approach to the store's design. The shop is easily visible from the lobby because of the open, double entryway.

HENRY'S

Amount Purchased
.50
$2
DESIGNERS
Professional Builder
Bon Appétit
Butterfinger
LIFE SAVERS
CERTS
Clorets
HALLS
Velamints
Trident
CLUB
Cheese Nips
TID-BIT
triscuit
RITZ

The curved, plexiglass lips on the display cases reinforce the circular theme of the shop. The central counter contains three presentation tiers on the top and two tiers on the bottom.

The rich, wood panel ceiling, dark wood displays and overhead canopy recall an old-world elegance and charm. The central counter is curved to soften the hard lines of the space. The modular wall units allow easy access to the merchandise.

B & L Patisserie Los Angeles, California

HONORABLE MENTION, Small Hard Goods Store under 6,000 Square Feet

Designer: Kenneth White Design Associates
Los Angeles, California

Functionality, Product Presentation and Atmosphere

Three key considerations influenced the development of a design for B & L Patisserie: functionality, product presentation and the creation of a unique atmosphere/identity.

Time and motion studies conducted at the shop's original location provided valuable insights into how the sales people work and how the public traffic flows. The experiences of being served and enjoying the fare at the patisserie had to be as effortless an experience as possible. Comfortably-spaced tables, counter and aisles accommodate the movement of both employees and customers.

The patisserie's products had to be visible and appealing, even though most of the pastries also had to be in cases and some refrigerated. This has been accomplished successfully through the selection of multi-shelved display cases that have a clean, crisp line and a minimum amount of distracting detail.

A Room Wrapped in *Trompe L'oeil* Drapery

The final step was to establish a distinctive atmosphere of lighthearted romance which would set this bakery apart from others. The white display cabinets are contrasted with the soft, warm cream *trompe l'oeil* that suggests gentle folds of drapery wrapping around the entire space. A blending of additional, interesting details—the Bacchus head wall sconces, the fresh, white table cloths, and the English lichen trees—completes a classically-romantic athmosphere that beckons the customer back.

Project:	B & L Patisserie
Location:	Los Angeles, California
Client:	Mr. & Mrs. Rudy Knoll
Design Firm:	Kenneth White Design Associates Los Angeles, California

INTERIOR DESIGN TEAM:

Planner:	Kenneth White, A.S.I.D., I.S.P.
Designers:	Kenneth White, A.S.I.D., I.S.P., James Trujillo, Associate Designer
Architect:	Cary Stevens
Project Manager:	Kenneth White, A.S.I.D., I.S.P.
President/Chairman:	Kenneth White, A.S.I.D., I.S.P.
Consultant:	Vincent Fama (lighting)
Contractor:	Ramco Builders (general)
Suppliers:	Team Ekistics (mural), David Jones (trees), Silvestri of California (sconces), ABC Letter Art (signage)
Photographer:	Milroy McAleer, Newport Beach, California

The distinct identity of the shop is achieved through the blending of unusual details, such as the walls adorned with *trompe l'oeil* draperies and the Bacchus wall sconces.

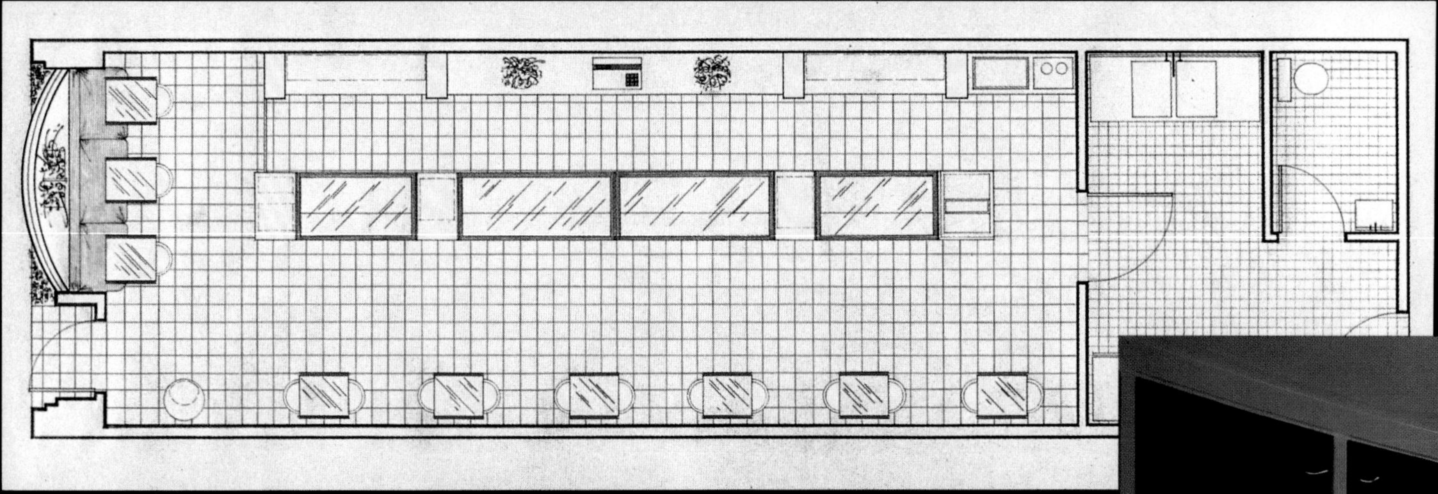

Subtle, pastel colors in the walls and furnishings soften the stark look of the white cabinets. Simple downlights are used over tables near the window.

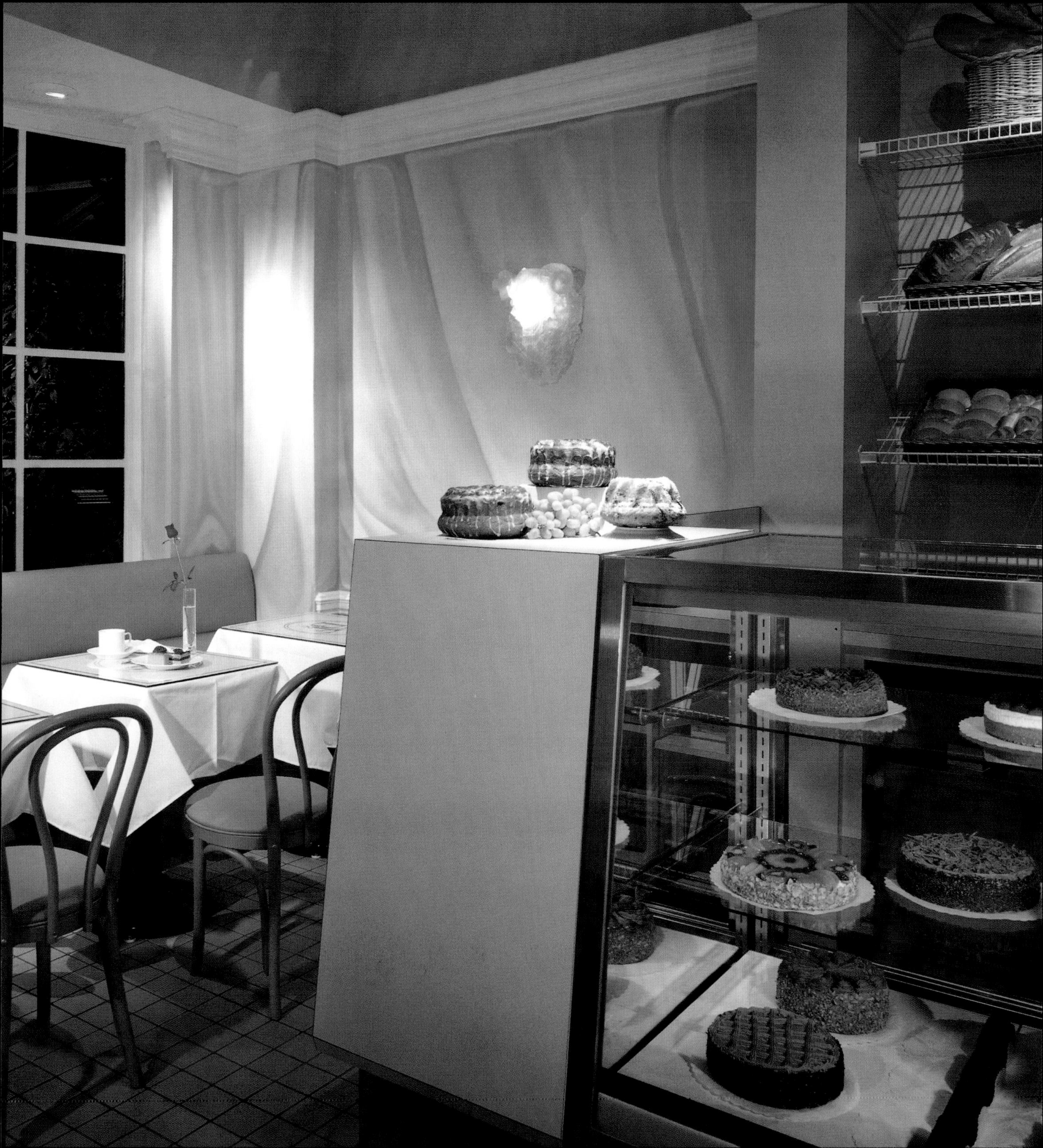

The large mirror behind the display counter makes the long, narrow space seem wider than it is. The English lichen trees add character to the neat, clean-lined shop.

Cabinets with glass tops and sides offer unobstructed views of the pastries. Customers and staff can move easily through the spacious aisles. Track lighting, painted an unobstrusive white, focuses attention on the mouth-watering pastries.

APPENDIX

The ISP/NRMA Store Interior Design Competition Rules And Requirements

Purpose

To promote recognition of the value of good design interiors. To recognize the contributions of particular organizations and individuals.

Entry Requirements

1. Stores must have been completed (opened for business) during the year previous to the competition date.
2. At least one member of the design team must be a current member of the Institute of Store Planners or have an application pending for membership.
3. Entries must be completed fully to the following instructions.
4. Only one submission is permitted per category per entrant.
5. Entries must be received prior to the end of the business day on October 15 of the previous year.

Return of Entries

1. All entries become the property of the Institute of Store Planners and the National Retail Merchants Association and will not be returned.
2. The Institute of Store Planners and the National Retail Merchants Association will be showing slides from this competition throughout the following year. Credits will be given to the store and the designers. If you wish your slides *not* to be used, please so indicate on the entry form.

Awards

1. One winner and two honorable mentions per category.
2. One store out of all the entries will be awarded "GRAND PRIZE".
3. Judges may change categories of individual entries if deemed appropriate.
4. Winning entries and honorable mentions will receive a certificate.
5. Winners in each category will receive an inscribed mounted plaque.
6. Awards will be presented by the ISP at the NRMA Store Planning, Design & Visual Merchandising Conference held in New York City. ISP members not participating in the conference can attend the presentation luncheon at the same price as the attendees. (Details of this event will be publicized separately.)
7. Award winners should be notified by November 1.

Jury

Judges of the competition include highly respected store designers, retailers, and academicians..

General Instructions

1. This is a concealed identification competition. Each entrant is responsible for ensuring that his name is placed on the registration form and nowhere else. Identification is controlled through the registration number which must be noted on all pages and all slides.
2. All entries must be in the 8½" x 11" format and inserted in a three ring binder as described herein.
3. Should an entry receive an award and be used for publication, all credits and other information will be taken from the registration form, project description, and other information contained in the entry. By submitting an entry, an entrant acknowledges that all information is accurate and that he has the right to publish this material.
4. These instructions may be used for entry to as many categories as desired by photocopying the registration form.
5. Entries should be packaged carefully and sent to:
   ISP/NRMA STORE INTERIOR DESIGN COMPETITION
   INSTITUTE OF STORE PLANNERS
   211 East 43rd Street, Suite 1601
   New York, NY 10017
   Entries must arrive before the end of the business day on October 15.

◆ **SPECIAL NOTE:** For best possible reproduction in a book of contest winners, be sure to submit ORIGINAL 35mm and larger format transparencies .

INDEX I
DESIGN FIRMS

INDEX II
DESIGNERS

INDEX III
DECORATORS

INDEX IV

CONTRACTORS / SUPPLIERS

for Retail Interior Designers . Store Planners . Display Managers . Commercial Architects . Visual Merchandise Directors . and anyone interested in visual marketing

The Best of Store Designs

STILL AVAILABLE

From the National Retail Merchants Association and the Institute of Store Planners' Annual Design Competition

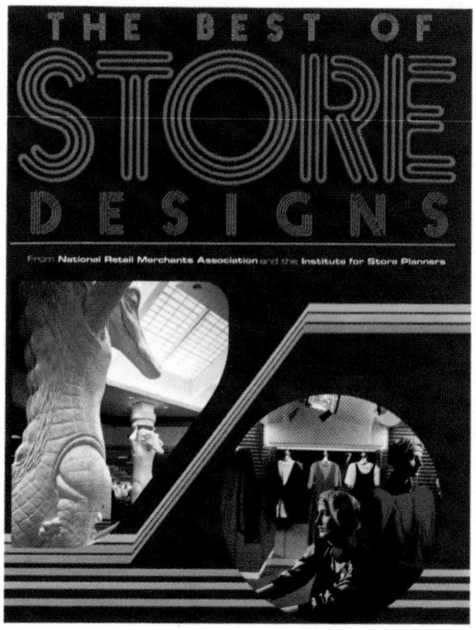

A new generation of affluent shoppers has sparked radical changes in the way retail stores are designed. The very best of these new designs are captured vividly in **The Best of Store Designs** in large, breathtaking photographs.

The winners of the annual NRMA/ISP retail store design competition are leaders of the new trends, using bold colors, and innovative treatments of fixtures and signage.

THE BEST OF
STORE DESIGNS
ISBN: 0-86636-012-3
Hardbound 9 x 12 in.
240 full-color pages
Over 100 photographs
and illustrations

The Best of Store Designs portrays the excitement generated by new designs and by renovations of department stores, hard goods retailers, specialty stores, and service establishments. Detailed text and captions give the background of each design and tells how it was executed. Credits list the store, the client, the designers, engineers, architects, fixtures suppliers, and interior designers.

Anyone who works with retail spaces will find **The Best of Store Designs** an essential guide to contemporary retail design.

The bold use of color, shapes, and new traffic patterns make **STORES** an indispensable guide to contemporary retail design.

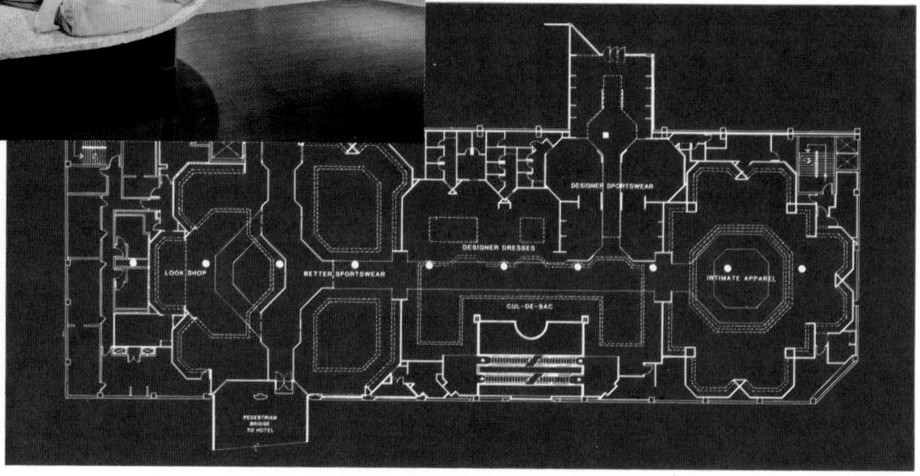

Actual floor plans show how the space was utilized for aisles, fixtures, storage, and selling area.

Available at bookstores and art supply centers, and from the publisher, PBC International, Inc., One School Street, Glen Cove, New York 11542.

for Retail Interior Designers · Store Planners · Display Managers · Commercial Architects · Visual Merchandise Directors · and anyone interested in visual marketing

The Best of Store Designs 2

from the National Retail Merchants Association and
the Institute of Store Planners' Store Interior Design Competition

THE BEST OF STORE DESIGNS 2
ISBN: 0-86636-015-8
Hardbound 9 × 12 in.
256 full-color pages
Over 200 illustrations, most in full color

The Best of Store Designs 2 is a vivid compilation of the winners of the 1985 ISP/NRMA Store Interior Design Competition sponsored by the prestigious Institute of Store Planners and the National Retail Merchants Association.

Springing from the success of the first book **The Best of Store Designs,** this edition is the second in what has already become an annual publishing event. The winners of this competition represent the leaders in retail design today. By creating new trends using colors, forms, and state-of-the-art fixtures, these stores have shown that good design pays. Winning designs from all store categories including full-line department stores to supermarket and convenience stores are showcased in 256 full-color pages.

Detailed text and captions give the background of each design, including the store, client, architect, interior design team, and other contractors such as lighting and signage suppliers.

Anyone interested in retail interior design, store planning, visual merchandising, or retail display will find **The Best of Store Designs 2** a valuable source of design ideas.

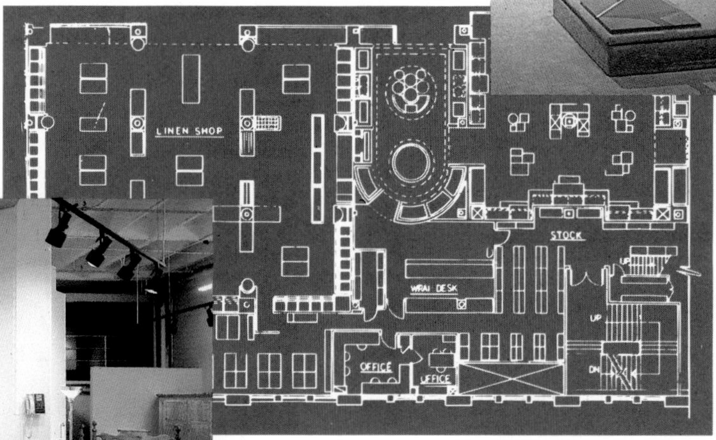

THE BEST OF STORE DESIGNS 2
shows the latest and best store designs with large, full-color photographs and detailed floor plans.

Available at bookstores and art supply centers, and from the publisher,
PBC International, Inc., One School Street, Glen Cove, New York 11542.

for Visual Merchandisers . Display Directors . Display Artists . Retailers . Store Planners . Visual Merchandise Managers . anyone involved in merchandise presentation

Visual Merchandising

Best Displays from Leading Designers

From the National Retail Merchants Association's Visual Merchandising Board of Directors

VISUAL MERCHANDISING
ISBN: 0-86636-014-X
Hardbound 9 x 12 in.
256 full-color pages
Over 400 full-color photographs

America's top merchandise display designers show their best work in VISUAL MERCHANDISING.

Innovative and exciting displays are essential for the rapid sales of products in today's department stores and boutiques.

Visual Merchandising is a compilation of the most current, dazzling, innovative merchandise display from America's top designers. Here is a valuable showcase of the latest and the best ideas for effective displays that help sell merchandise in a retail environment.

Compiled from the work of the National Retail Merchants Association's **(NRMA)** Visual Merchandising Board of Directors, the book is an essential reference for designers and anyone wishing to keep abreast of current trends.

All of the NRMA'S Visual Merchandising Board of Directors are represented with large full-color photos of their latest designs.

Some of the top designers and their stores featured in VISUAL MERCHANDISING are:

Tom Azzarello	Emporium Capwell
Robert Benzio	Saks Fifth Avenue
Cecil Bessellieu	Belk Stores
Linda Bramlage	Jordon Marsh Company
Frank Calise	Bonwit Teller
Joseph Feczko	Duty-Free Shoppers
Thomas R. Jewell	JC Penney Company, Inc.
Robert J. Mahoney	Gump's
Andrew J. Markopoulus	Dayton Hudson Department Stores
Rick McClelland	Jordon Marsh, Florida
Tom V. Natalini	Allied Stores Corporation
Ron Nelson	Z.C.M.I.
Angela Patterson	Bergdorf Goodman
Alan Petersen	John Wanamaker
Joseph Powers	Bamberger's
Steve Rix	Maas Brothers
Homer Sharp	Marshall Fields
Jim Seigler	Foley's
Tom Speedling	Naval Retail Service Support Office
Ken Spikes	Cain-Sloan
Jay Thompson	Bonwit Teller

Available at bookstores and art supply centers, and from the publisher, PBC International, Inc., One School Street, Glen Cove, New York 11542.